Racundra's Third Cruise

www.fernhurstbooks.co.uk

The Arthur Ransome Society was founded in 1990 with the aim of promoting interest in Arthur Ransome and his books. For more information on the Society visit their website at **www.arthur-ransome.org/ar**

In 1997 members of the Society formed The Nancy Blackett Trust with the intention of purchasing and restoring one of Ransome's own yachts, the Nancy Blackett, and using her to inspire interest in the books and to encourage young people to take up sailing. She now visits many classic boat shows around the country.

To find out more about the trust, or to contribute to the upkeep of the Nancy Blackett please write to the Nancy Blackett Trust (reg.charity1065058) at Sylvan Cottage, White House Walk, Farnham, Surrey, GU9 9AN or visit their website at **www.nancyblackett.org**

Racundra's Third Cruise

by Arthur Ransome

Including many original photographs
and sketches by the author

Edited and compiled by Brian Hammett

Text and pictures © The Arthur Ransome Literary Estate
Introduction © Brian Hammett

First published 2002 by Fernhurst Books,
Duke's Path, High Street, Arundel, West Sussex, BN18 9AJ, England

British Library Cataloguing in Publication Data.
A catalogue record for this book is available from the British Library

ISBN 1 898660 89 1

Printed in China through World Print

Artwork by Creative Byte

Cover design by Simon Balley

For a free, full-colour brochure write, phone, fax or email us:

Fernhurst Books, Duke's Path, High Street,
Arundel, West Sussex BN18 9AJ, United Kingdom
Phone: 01903 882277
Fax: 01903 882715
Email: sales@fernhurstbooks.co.uk
Website: www.fernhurstbooks.co.uk

Contents

Introduction
by Brian Hammett

This account of the third cruise of Arthur Ransome's famous yacht *Racundra*, from Riga to Mitau via the River Aa, was written by Ransome himself but has not hitherto been published - even though the cruise took place between August 1st and September 10th 1924 - now nearly 80 years ago. Ransome himself clearly intended to publish it but did not complete his 80-page typescript beyond the story of the first 23 days. There follows a gap in his typed account of eleven days, two days in which he types up his notes of the sad episode during which his wife abandons ship and a further gap of five days during which he returned Racundra to her home berth leaving only his deck-log. Full acknowledgements of the relevant Ransome sources are given at the end of the book.

We do not know why he failed to complete to actual publication or, indeed, when he prepared the manuscript to the stage that he did. We know that at this time he was commissioned to write a series of articles, which took priority. Perhaps he was not satisfied with it, although there is no evidence for this. Ransome spent much time on the cruise itself in writing his articles for the Manchester Guardian and indulging in his passion for fishing but it seems likely that he had publication in mind from the start since in addition to his diary and the brief 'real-time' deck-log that he kept, as all cruising sailors must, he kept a separate daily summary and amplifying details. These three sources together with some handwritten notes and drafts of his typescript provide a detailed full account of the cruise.

The narrative contains a blow by blow and fish by fish daily account of the trip with much to interest the sailor, fisherman and traveller alike. The handwritten essay on The Apothecary of Wolgund is a forerunner of Ransome's later style of writing and of particular interest. The account of Racundra's Third Cruise (Racundra Goes Inland) is reproduced exactly as originally written, apart from a few very minor corrections of typographical errors. The following fonts are used throughout: Ransome's typescript in American Typewriter, his handwriting in *Baskerville Semi Bold Italic,* and extracts form published material in Times New Roman. In the 1920s many of the locations mentioned had different names.

The interest in preparing this publication came from an article in Mixed Moss, the journal of the Arthur Ransome Society, in which Alan Lawrence describes retracing Ransome's cruise up the river Lieupe (Aa) from Riga to Jelgrava (Mitau) a distance of some 45 miles.

The major part of the narrative comes from the typescript 'Racundra Goes Inland'.

The relevant passages from Ransome's diary, deck log and notes have been included at the start of each day's writing. Some of the typescript comes from what Ransome refers to as his 'small book'. Where this occurs it is labelled as such.

The voyage took place within a few years of the end of hostilities in the Baltic at a time when place names were still mainly in German. Nowadays they have reverted to the original local language:

Formerly	Currently	Formerly	Currently
Aa	Lieupe	Mitau	Jelgrava
Bilderlingshof	Jurmala	New Dubbeln	Jaindubulti
Bolderaa	Buijupe	Pawassern	Pavasan
Bruwer	Bruver	Plerren	Planciem
Dirbe	Kalnciems	Ratneek	Rutas
Dubbeln	Dubulti	Reval	Tallin
Dvina	Daugava	St. Joanna	Spunnciems
Frankendorf	Likumciems	Schaggern	Sipolciems
Grasche	Gulbjuciems	Scholk	Sloka
Helsingfors	Helsinki	Selme Oding	Upmaji
Kaling	Gate	Umul	Pavieda
Kalnzeem	Tirji	Waltershof	Valteri
Kesa	Slokas	Wolgund	Valgrunde

Racundra, of course, could not have her third cruise without earlier having her second, and before that her first. Before that, Ransome had to have the dream, she had to be designed, and she had to be built. Details of this period prior to the writing of Racundra's Third Cruise, together with more of Ransome's unpublished work relating to the period, are included at the end of this volume.

Arthur Ransome.

Evgenia Shelepina.

Racundra's Third Cruise
(Racunda Goes Inland)
By Arthur Ransome

Sept. 1   *-Ditto-*
    2   *-Ditto-*
    3   *-Ditto-*
    4   *Exit of Cook. New Dubbeln.*
    5   *New Dubbeln - Bilderlingshof.*
    6   *Bullen - Bilderlingshof.*
    7   *Bilderlingshof - Babit. S. W.*
    8   *Babit. S. W. - Mitau.*
    9   *Mitau - Bilderlingshof.*
   10   *Bilderlingshof to Bolderaa & Dvina to Stint Sea.*

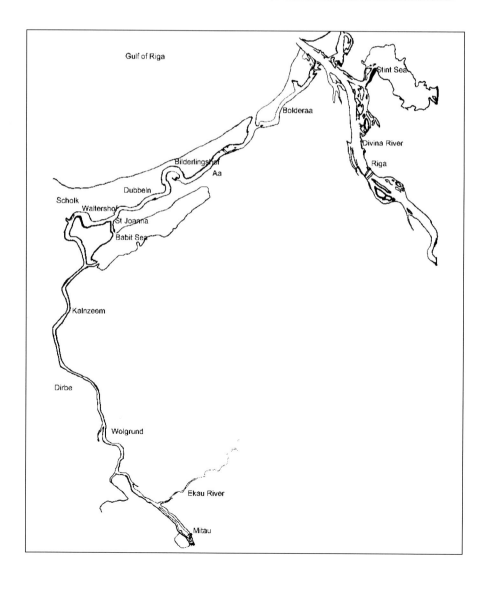

RACUNDRA GOES INLAND

Friday August 1st   Sailed to Bolderaa.

(Diary)   *Sailed. Anchored in Bolderaa.*
          Under power
(Log)   *Friday. Anchored at Bolderaa.*
          Morning fishing with rain under pier.
          Old man catching ersh.

Got away under motor from the Little Harbour, the Ancient
insisting on being on board at the start. His little double-ended
dinghy towed from the mizzen shrouds and he, proud pilot of his
tiny port, conned us out, stowed the anchor chain for the last
time, and, when we were fairly out into the lake, shook hands,
wished us a good trip, and dropped over the side. His dinghy
was scarcely a cable's length astern when the engine hesitated
a little in its panting run, coughed once or twice, seemed to have
swallowed a plum stone, and stopped. I could feel the old man,
as he rested on his oars, thinking to himself that without him
on board we should be in trouble at once. I think he had never
quite forgiven us our voyage from Reval to Riga in the early
spring. I lashed the tiller amidships and dropped down the
companion to see what I could do to help the little donkey. You
see by now I had lost all my hate for him, and was sure that
he was doing his best. I did him no injustice. The fault was mine.
I had forgotten to open the cock of the lubricator, and the poor
little creature was over hot. It was lucky that he had had the
sense to stop when he did. I opened the cock and further moved
the regulator to allow a much larger than usual quantity of oil
to go through, and then, while he was still hot, started him
again. He made no show of resistance but went off again as well
as he could, protesting only gently that if I ran him at full speed
before the oil had got properly into his circulation he would be
in trouble again. So I set him to go very slow, and went on deck
again. The Cook was still stowing provisions in the cabin. The
Ancient was still resting on his oars watching us, waiting, I knew,
for a hail of distress. When he saw us again on our course, be laid
to his oars, though softly, and had not disappeared into his little
harbour before we were more than half way down the lake, and
were turning the promontory of tall reeds that hid him from us.

The couple of sticks that mark the channel through the shallows

*A big Swede passed us
and I wished his course were ours.*

into the Mühlgraben were gone, but that did not trouble us so
much as a tug coming out with four barges tandem that were
bound to swing at the sharp turn in the channel. However,
though they did swing, we got past with a few yards to spare,
and were presently passing two Norwegians coaling in the
Mühlgraben, and a German, loading timber. At the corner where
the Red Dvina leads to the island where Racundra was built,
opposite the little pier to which we had tied up while waiting
in vain for the Customs officials in the spring, were four sailing
vessels, three schooners and a cutter, making a fine picture, but
unfortunately with the sun behind then an impossible one for
the camera. We passed on down the Mühlgraben, avoiding fishing
nets and little fishing boats, and so out into the great Dvina
River, as if we were once more bound for the sea. A big Swede
passed us going down the river and I wished his course were
ours, and that we were taking Racundra out again to her proper
home, to the big seas that she rides so easily, to the big winds
that she was built for, and days and nights of steady sailing
out of the smell of the land. But we turned for the first time
to the left bank of the river and, near the mouth of it, round
a conical beacon and into what is known as the Bolderaa which
joins the Dvina and the Courland Aa. The Aa has its own outlet
into the sea at Bullen, but the channel is shifting and unmarked,
and steamers invariably come into the Aa from the Dvina.

An opening railway bridge crosses the Bolderaa, and as we
approached it I dropped down the companion, reduced the engine
to slowest speed and jumped on deck again. A passenger steamer

We turned into what is known as the Bolderaa.

passed us. A green painted cargo steamship was coming up astern. The bridge was closed. The passenger steamer hooted for all of us, and just as she reached the bridge it swung open and she passed through. I jumped down again and asked the little donkey for all he could give us, and, making an important little fuss with his full eight hundred revolutions we slipped through the bridge just ahead of the green steamer and, with the respect of little for big, got out of her way on the other side, knowing well that the steamers in the Aa do not love yachts and given any excuse to put them in the wrong enjoy making the most of it. So, though Racundra was the overtaken vessel, she gathered her skirts and got onto the pavement, or into the shallow water, while the big green cargo steamer wallowed past her with a wave that sent things rattling in the galley, and brought a protest from the Cook, who thought I was throwing her about in play.

It was already growing dusk, but I knew we could anchor anywhere if we could only find deep enough water out of the steamer track, and presently with lead on deck we began to feel our way. We could see the shallower patches by the weeds just breaking the surface, and we steered between them with a wide stretch of water on either side, broken by reed beds. Wild duck were flying overhead, and it was hard to believe we were only a few miles from the town. There was no wind. On the northern shore I saw a log built hut and a timber built pier, with a few more huts among some low trees. That looks like milk for tomorrow's porridge, thought I, and sounding with the lead took Racundra towards the reed beds and anchored in a fathom and a half. There were reed beds on each side of us, east and west, so that we were well out of the channel, but I put the riding light on the forestay, and we had supper and a game of bezique and so to bed.

Saturday August 2nd   Bilderlingshof.

(Diary)   *Early morning fished in rain, sheltered under wooden pier with an old man catching ersh with a paternoster with a two foot rod.*

Sailed under power to Bilderlingshof.

Had long wait to go through bridge.
Anchored by yachts to the side.
When no milk to shop and back.

Esti motor yacht drifted across our bows.

(Log)   *Saturday. Steamed to Bilderlingshof.*
Waiting for road and train bridge.
Anchored out of stream by yachts.
Esthonians motor boat waiting for bridge developed attachment with our hawser.

Early in the morning I went fishing in the dinghy close by the old timber pier and was presently joined there by an old man in a boat which he insinuated between the piles and so got completely inside the pier. I caught nothing but a few small perch, and presently it began to rain, and I too, slipped my dinghy under the pier and was able to watch the old man. He was fishing with paternosters, small weights at the end of his lines, and the hooks attached a little a little way above them, and he was catching ersh. The ersh is a little fish rather like a gudgeon but with a big prickly fin on his back like that of a perch. He is never more than a few inches in length and he is greatly prized for the making of soup to which he imparts a relish given by no other fish. The old man was fishing with three or four lines at once, attached to little rods about eighteen inches or two feet long, fastened to the gunwale of his boat. When a fish bit, the end of the little rod dipped and the old

We sailed under power to Bilderlingshof.

man hauled up the line hand over hand as fast as he could. He was evidently accustomed to fishing in this place, for all his paternoster lines were tied to the ends of his little slips of rods, and were of exactly the right length. He had but to the throw them out and they were just taut to the tips of the rods when the weights rested on the bottom. Presently the wind came gently from the west, then harder, in gusts, and with it white squalls of rain over the water. The planks of the pier were open over my head, and I began to get very wet indeed, even when holding the boat so as to get as much shelter as possible from one of the main beams. "If this gets much worse," said the old man, "we shall not be able to stay even here and we shall get very wet going home. Will you just have a look out and see if more clouds are coming up?" Reaching up and pulling on the planks of the pier with my hands so that water poured down my sleeves I pulled the nose of the boat out and looked round. It was certainly lightening a little but I could see more white squalls coming with black water glittering and foaming as the rain poured down into it with a hissing noise that you could hear long before the squall reached you. I told the old man. He was hauling up ersh one after another, and his conversation was divided between me and the fish. "More rain coming. Well I am in better shelter than you, though not good enough. That's a fine one. That's a lively fellow. Is it clearing a little now? Ha, my beauty. Up you come. More rain. Ah well it must stop sometime. Best of the day, you are. Into the bucket with you. The fishing here? There was a man caught an eight pound eel, and I have caught a two pounder myself. Now would you just look out

The Cook steered.

again?" It cleared at last, and the old man, quite dry, paddled
away with his booty, while I, soaked to the skin went to
Racundra and got the milk can, took it ashore, got fresh
milk from a woman who talked good Russian at the log hut,
and returned to the ship to find coffee and porridge ready.

After breakfast we started away under motor. The Cook steered
and I stood on the foredeck watching for weed patches under
water. We found to our astonishment that we were hardly
moving through the water. The little donkey seemed to have
relapsed to its sullen ca'canny of last year and my good will
towards it weakened, until the Cook, peering over the stern
announced that we had a little haystack instead of a propeller
and that our propeller was not to be seen at all. We decided to
crawl on with it so, and to anchor by Bilderlingshof and set
about diving operations to clear it up. We must have gone
through a weed bed in the dusk last night and the propeller
had gathered to itself all that was good for it and more.
It was not the little donkey's fault. This was his, as ours,
first experience of weed beds and inland sailing.

Two men, after duck, slipped close along the edge of the reeds
in a green canoe-like punt. One paddled in the stern, the other
sat, with his gun across his knees a little forward of midships.
We had scarcely passed them before we heard a shot and looking
back saw a duck pulled up suddenly in mid air, turning over
and falling in a muddle of wings, all purpose gone, into the
reeds, while another, flying desperately fast, and rising all

*The reeds opened and we could see a broad pathway of
water leading to the open sea.*

the time, fled terrified far over our heads.

The channel was not difficult, for in the shallow places the weeds
made patches of smooth water, but we took turns now that it
was too late, in standing on the foredeck to watch for weeds
under water. We passed close by some fishermen, setting pike
traps, and then to the north of us the reeds opened and we could
see a broad pathway of water leading to the open sea. Far out we
could see a steamship heading north on the old course to Finland
that we now feel we know by heart. Even now, for a moment, we
were tempted to pick our way out by that channel and abandon
our inland expedition, but memory of the trouble we should get
into for going to sea without clearing at the Customs, and of
the fact that this would perhaps be our last chance of going up
a beautiful and little known river kept us wise, and we left the
pathway to the sea astern of us and headed now south east
down a broad stretch of the Aa river, with pine forests on high
banks behind the reeds. We turned west again with the river and
in doubt as to which side of an island to pass chose the northern
side and had scarcely done so when we saw a steamer take the
southern channel. However, I had the lead on deck and found
plenty of water, and, we steamed on until within sight of the
railway bridge at Bilderlingshof, when seeing fish rising close
along the shore, we decided that this would be a good anchorage
from which we could observe the procedure with the bridge,
clean our propeller and possibly catch some perch for soup.

We dealt with the propeller first, cleaning away what we could
of the haystack with a boat-hook. Then I went overboard and
under water and finished the job by hand. It was little wonder
that we had been hardly moving and I am still in doubt as to

It is a combined road and railway bridge.

why we went forward instead of backward or simply standing still; the propeller was a solid ball of waterlily stems and flat ribbon-like weed. Boats are very responsive to intention. In a flat calm, I remember setting a straight course from Roogö to Baltic Port in Kittiwake, and, with sails flapping idly, somehow got there without using the sweeps. We had told the engine what we wanted. The engine had told the propeller, and the propeller, while embarrassed by the over effusive embraces of the weeds, must have whispered to them that, this was all very well, but, that they must let the boat keep moving or he would get into trouble for tolerating followers during working hours. After drying in the cockpit I took the dinghy to try for perch, but got none worth keeping. And as for the bridge, we could make nothing of it. It is a combined road and railway bridge. There were signals on it which changed from time to time but clearly did not correspond to its opening or shutting. No yachts approached it. Steamers came up, hooting loudly and a section of it swung open to let them pass. So, in the afternoon we took the foghorn on deck, got the anchor up, started the little donkey and steamed boldly for the bridge. A train chose that moment to cross it, so we slowed down and waited till it had passed. Then, heading straight for the opening section, we hooted as if steamer-born. Nothing happened. Remembering how in Holland, swing bridges delight in opening so late as to flick flies from the bowsprits of yachts coming through, and unwilling to betray any nervousness or lack of faith, feeling that this would encourage indifference or hostility in the bridge-keeper as it does in strange dogs, we held boldly on. Nothing happened. At the very last moment we swung Racundra's head round, made a wide circle and approached the bridge again. Nothing happened. The bridge-keeper, arms folded, watched us with mild inactive interest as if we were waltzing for the public benefit. The hooting of our little

Waltzing for the public benefit.

foghorn stirred no responsive chord. We might have been a stout and stately swallow gyrating after flies. Then a cargo steamer came up the river. Now, at least, we thought, they will open the bridge. The cargo steamer hooted. Nothing happened, and the cargo steamer elbowed herself alongside a little wooden jetty and tied up. I dropped below and reduced the little donkey to slow speed. I dared not anchor again, for at any minute I might find the proper "Open Sesame" the bridge would open and close again before we had got through. So we went on with our steady but impatient dance. Another steamer came up, this time a big passenger steamer for Mitau, hooted with the rest or us, shut off her engines, drifted a moment or two and presently tied up alongside the cargo steamer. And still the bridge-keeper did nothing. Now and again he changed the signals and allowed a motor or a train to cross his bridge. (Both cannot, it seems, pass at once.) We had been waltzing for an hour when suddenly we saw the passenger steamer cast off. We hurried up the donkey but as ill luck would have it, the bridge opened when we were at the further end of our orbit, and both steamers were through and the bridge keeper was, after keeping us waiting all this time, actually beckoning to us to come on, before we slipped through.

It was now evening. Half a dozen yachts were lying at anchor off Bilderlingshof, so, choosing a vacant berth well out of the line of the steamers and giving us room to swing between the shore and the last yacht we anchored for the night. The Bilderlingshof on the river Aa is as it were the back door to the Bilderlingshof on the shore of the sea. The one has white painted restaurants, a Casino, flamingly dressed bathers and all the most expensive clothes that the richest shopkeepers of Riga can afford to buy. The other is a settlement of little wooden houses with mud streets winding between them under the pine trees. I do not think anyone can have wasted any paint on the houses there since the war. It is quite a likeable little place and the little houses, which have small unkempt gardens behind wooden palings, no two like each other, each with its rough boat fastened to a stake outside, are the sort of little houses I would not mind living in if I had not got Racundra. There were several things we had forgotten to buy and I went ashore and after losing myself in the little winding alleyways came through a backyard into an open space and found a village shop, a real village shop selling matches, sticky sweets, cigarettes, bad pipe tobacco, milk, meat, flour, vegetables and smoked fish. I bought some of these things and returned to the ship to put up our riding light, though I did not think there was need for it and trimmed it and set it on the forestay just to pretend to myself that I was a stickler for routine. I was wrong. Even here there was need for a riding light, although the having one did not save us as it should have done. About ten or eleven o'clock, when it was quite dark, a yacht and two steamers were waiting, as we had waited, for the bridge to open to let them through going the other way. I watched to see what would happen and presently heard a man in a boat say that the bridge would be open at eleven. Just then a very fast, large motor launch came down the river, also expecting to go through. I got a glimpse of her as she passed and thought I recognised her for a boat I had seen at Reval.

They had a strong searchlight on board with which they searched the river, and two women on board stood in the light of their own searchlight for the benefit of the people on shore. There was shouting and singing on board her. They went twice down to the bridge and then took a wide curve up the river again. I went below and to bed and was just turning in when I heard voices close aboard us and tumbled up as fast as I could to find the big motor launch, her engines shut off, drifting down close upon us. Our light was burning and they had absolutely no excuse. Apparently they were simply anxious to save petrol by not keeping their engines going while waiting for the bridge, and, at the same time were unwilling to drop a kedge. They were Esthonians from the Reval Yacht Club. They drifted broadside on across our bows, said it did not matter when I hailed them, and I had to prevent a collision and save their propeller from my own anchor chain by hurriedly letting out a lot of chain. They finally drifted past, one man of the many on board taking sufficient interest in proceedings to help with his feet in fending

off. We felt a good deal happier when the bridge had opened and
closed behind them, and I remembered the remark of another
member of that club when I asked him when he was putting to
sea. "I have not got enough spirits." "But I thought yours was
a sailing vessel." "So she is."

Sunday August 3rd   Dubbeln, St. Johanna.

(Diary)   *Found water over floorboards. Leak from*
           reversing screw.
           Put it right.
           Under motor to Dubbeln. Anchored & fished.
           Then under sail with S.E. wind, lovely sunset,
           to just beyond St Johanna.

(Log)   *Sunday. Under motor to above Dubbeln. Water*
           over floorboards. Nut off reversing joint.
           Anchored and fished.
           Then four miles sail. Wind S.E. Grazing cows.
           Evening thunder clouds in S.E. & S.W. Sunset.
           Old mill. Farmwoman milking cows. Forests.
           People fishing in creeks by St Johanna.
           Tried to anchor near the right bank. Very deep
           close to edge.
           Crossed to left bank. Anchored in three fathoms.

I tumbled up early in the morning and into a minor panic on
finding the water over the floorboards. This is a thing that never
happens on Racundra. We pump her out once or twice in a cruise
but only from politeness, never from staring necessity like this.
Brave men like E. F. Knight can cross the North Sea in a thirty
foot ketch that needs pumping every two hours, but we, merely
navigating the Aa river, felt the ground cut away from under our
feet, our whole trust in life undermined, the central article of our
creed destroyed at a blow by some inhuman agnostic. "Racundra
does not leak". We have gone to bed with that belief and waked
with it for two years, and now this morning there was the water
slopping about over the floorboards, so that the cooking had to
be done barefoot. I rigged the pump that I had fixed up this year
in Reval (in previous years we had no fixed pump but a garden
syringe and a bucket) and found it rusted solid. It is a little
circular force pump. I took off the india-rubber tubes, shoved

*A little indifferent tug thumped its slow way
with regular blows.*

a beer cork into the lower orifice, and filled it with paraffin. Half and hour later, with the water perceptibly deeper, I had another go at it. The handle moved only half an inch each way at first, but soon recovered its full swing. I let out the kerosene, rerigged the tubing, poured a little water into the pump and in a minute had the profound satisfaction of hearing the water sluicing over the side as I sat on the motor box and pumped. I pumped her practically dry, and listened. Sure enough I could hear a steady trickling somewhere in the stern. I took the companion steps, which form the motor box, away and saw at once whence came the water. It was pouring in with a steady stream through the propeller tube. The brass nut at the hither end of the reversing apparatus (the propeller revolves always in one direction and reverses by feathering its blades) had worked loose and was hanging free on the propeller shaft. I twisted myself snake-like round the engine, and screwed it in with a spanner. The leak stopped. That was all. Our creed was re-established. The agnostic had fooled us for a moment by misquotation of a text. We had now triumphantly confuted him.

The only question was, had I by screwing in that nut done anything to impede the engine? Engineers would laugh at such a question but I was making friends with my donkey slowly and with diffidence. You will remember that for the whole of the first year we had never thought we should be friends. Well, we could answer that question by starting the donkey, and, in the glow of confidence given by the stopping of the leak I made a new experiment, and instead of starting the donkey with the noisy blow-lamp, I tried the little hot cartridges which, lit by fuses, engender such a heat that in thirty seconds the engine is eager to begin. There is a trick about these things, and you have to pick your moment exactly if you are to start away with the use of one cartridge. I used two. I have always had to use two except on one happy occasion, when the donkey started with the first cartridge, filling me with so much pride that the Cook said it would be better for my character if I were never to try to do it with one cartridge again. The donkey, as I say, settled down to work after the second cartridge. I got the anchor on board and we steamed away from Bilderlingshof on a glorious sunny morning, fishermen in their little boats clustered at every likely reed patch, and a few racing yachts moving miraculously in an imaginary wind. The shore of the river here rises on one side into steep pine-covered cliffs, with here and there flat meadow with wooden farms, and on the other side little wooden houses like those of Bilderlingshof. Then the little wooden summer houses end, and you are sailing through pasturelands on one side and forest on the other, though the forest is but a strip along the high land that separates the river from the invisible Babit Lake. Then, by Kuevenhof the river bends in a horseshoe north and then south again, and in the turn of the horseshoe you are in civilization of a kind once more, the ugly civilization of factory and summer resort, a band making a noise somewhere, rowing boats out on hire painted red, white and blue, a forgotten survival of the old Russian colours, steamboat piers, and rowdy people. Even here the real life of the river persists, and along one shore were immense areas of floated timber, and through the crowd of Sunday trippers, a little indifferent tug thumped its slow way with regular blows, churning the water astern of it, but moving slowly, so slowly, towing an immense raft of logs, a couple of hundred yards long, with tents of the lumbermen on board and the lumbermen with their long poles moving on the logs, a few of them cooking at a little fire close by their tent, having come with the logs from the distant forests up the river where they grew together with their trees.

The railway station on the Riga railway is here on the very bank of the river, and for that reason, as the Cook had to go to Riga for the day on the Monday, we thought of stopping there and, steaming on to the southern corner of the horseshoe and beyond all the noise and flurry of the holidaymakers to a reedy bend with a waterlily bay that looked as if it might hold perch, we stopped the donkey, and anchored while we went with our fishing rods in the dinghy to see what we could find. We found poorish fishing, and, towards the end of the afternoon, when a southeasterly breeze got up, we decided to go further, even if that meant a longer walk from our anchorage to the railway. We got the sail up and went on another four miles up the river, with the great relief of not hearing the chatter of the little donkey. I suppose the little donkey does not make much noise as little donkeys go, but he makes enough to prevent us hearing each other without shouting when I am on the foredeck and the Cook is in the steering well. We have to signal steering directions when going through weed patches and even when we are both in the steering well, conversation is altogether impossible. Also the little fellow is so persistent. He just goes on, hammering at our tympanums, and the repetition of his sturdy little blows, when he is doing his eight hundred revolutions to the minute, brings about in the end a sort of desperation. The wind was not much of a wind but we slid along in silence and that in itself was a delight.

Also this stretch of the river above Dubbeln is one of the loveliest on the river. The left bank is broken; here and there the forest comes to the water's edge. Here and there are broad water meadows with grazing cattle and the forest behind them, with little wooden houses tucked under the trees. The right bank in places has been undercut and carved by the spring floods and the out-rush of ice after the winter into low sandy cliffs. Here and there dunes rise as if on the shores of an ancient sea, and these dunes are not bare but covered with pines. Then, towards St. Johanna, on the left bank the woods recede and there are meadows, whereas on the right bank the forest comes up to the river banks, hiding in its outskirts the little wooden houses that one can only see after one has learnt where to look for them by seeing a boat or two tied to a post or a tiny boat landing. The wind fell away as we approached St. Johanna, which we knew by the little three-corner spire of a church among the trees. Men were fishing in the waterlily creeks on that side of the river, and, where a farm lay by the riverbank, a dairymaid had taken her milking stool into the meadow instead of bringing the cows home, and was milking them by the riverbank.

We sailed slowly on towards a rich crimson sunset and its reflection and the reflection of the weeds in the water that was scarcely stirred by the wind. The sun set. For a minute or two there was a dead calm and we were thinking of waking up the donkey when the wind came again, scattered the reflections in a moment and made us busy with the sails. Just beyond St. Johanna the river makes a sharp double bend, to the south and then to the west again. In the first of these corners coming from the east is a steamer pier, and the village of Waltershof, almost entirely hidden by the trees, a fine sweep of tall reeds, and big beds of water lilies, a good place for perch as it

*This stretch of the river above Dubbeln
is one of the loveliest.*

afterwards proved. In the second bend we saw a farmhouse on
the bank, and high dunes covered with pines. It seemed to promise alike milk and good shelter, and we left Waltershof and sailed
on, fast enough now into this second bend. Right in the corner,
close by the farm I began to ply the lead and found six or
seven fathoms. Nearer and nearer to the bank we came and the
depth scarcely lessened. We were closing quickly with the reeds.
Expecting shallower water we had come so near that it was
clear that we should not have room to swing on the scope of
chain necessary to give our anchor a grip. I doubted if there
was room even to go about. Things were happening a good deal
faster than I can tap them out on the typewriter. I took one
more sounding. It was clear that the river had hollowed this
bend out to the very shores. So I dropped the anchor to help
her head round. This just did it. We swung and caught the
wind in time to draw off again with her mizzen boom already
among the reeds, and the hard shallows like a wall, appearing
suddenly a foot or two from the stern. The moment she had
the wind again I had the anchor off the ground once more and,
in the rapidly deepening dusk we fled away back to the first
bend and the waterlily bay of Waltershof. Here I found three
fathoms shallowing to two just out of the line of steamers
approaching the pier from up river, and in two and a half
fathoms we anchored.

In two and a half fathoms we anchored.

Monday August 4th to Wednesday August 6th St. Johanna.

(Diary, Mon) *E. Went to town.*

Typed 'Money Reform'.

Caught small pike from Racundra.

(Log) *Monday Cook went to town. I typed 'Money Reform' and caught a small pike from Racundra's deck bringing him unceremoniously on board.*
Night wind S.E.

(Diary, Tues) *Fished in rain.*

(Diary, Weds) *Wind veering to S.W. Rain.*

Posted 'Money Reform" to M.G.

Caught a good perch & others.

(Log) *Weds. Persistent rain often. Wind E. Caught mainly perch. Perch soup.*

At St. Johanna

In the morning when there was light enough to look about us we
found our anchorage a good deal better than I had imagined it
when worrying about it in the dark. Our stern swung easily clear
of the weeds visible under water and we were clear also of the
steamer track to the little pier at Waltershof because to the south
of us there was a long promontory of reeds, which kept the
steamers away from us. Tugs and rafts going down stream and not
stopping at Waltershof passed far away on the other side of the
bend. From our corner of the double bend of the river there was
little water to be seen. It was as if we were in a lake, and when
I looked out in the early morning it was quite surprising to see the
mast and port lights of a steamer moving through the blue mist
apparently on dry land further down the river. Opposite us, where
we had tried to anchor last night was a snug little farm under the
pines and presently I hoisted the sail in the dinghy and set out on
my usual morning expedition to find milk for the porridge. The
farm proved a disappointment. I should have been three hours
earlier to get milk, for here as almost everywhere along the river,
all the milk it put through separating machines, so that the inferior
milk of towns and the cream for which a high price is paid may
be sent down stream to Riga. The people at the farm were
unsympathetic, being fully occupied with the building of a new
house, and it was owing to the kindness of one of their workmen
that I learnt that milk could be got at the village lying in the trees
behind the pier at Waltershof. I sailed over there in the dinghy and
got some machine-made milk, but on my way back to the boat was
stopped by a fisherman who said he had a cow of his own and if I
liked to call in the morning I could get real milk from him. I found
an excellent little shop where we could replenish our paraffin tanks
and buy beer and local tobacco. More serious provisioning could not
be done here and the Cook decided to go to Riga for the day,
because the railway at this point is only a mile from the river and
if we were going to the Babit Lake, we should be wholly out of
touch with such things. So holding a council, we decided to stay
here a day or two while I finished some work I had to do. Racundra
is for me a floating study, not merely a holiday boat, and cruising
has always to give way before the more serious needs of earning
bread and butter with a little jam. So I sailed the Cook to the
steamer pier and then settled down to work and finished an article
and was in the middle of the rough draft of a second when
I was interrupted by a mild splash, splash quite close to the boat.
I made sure it was a small pike, and so put a bait out on a single
hook and a small float and went on with my writing in the cockpit.
The float drifted round towards the reeds and there stayed just
clear of them for a minute or two and then slid quietly under and
moved round in a wide circle just below the surface of the water.

*We eventually anchored
a little way below a raft bridge.*

Two minutes later a small pike joined me in the cockpit. The little
fellow was not worth keeping but he was enough to encourage me
to fish there, and on the Tuesday and Wednesday besides work,
the Cook and I fished hard, mostly under rain, but caught no more
pike, though on Wednesday night we had an admirable perch
soup for our supper. The perch, however, caught on worm, did
not run large and we promised ourselves better sport when we
should reach the Babit.

Thursday August 7th   N. Entrance of Babit.

(Diary)   *Moored at entrance to Babit*

           Anchored in 7 fathom.

(Log)   *Thursday. Shifted to entrance to Babit.*
           Family of 3 Germans with 14 pike rods
           caught one 3 pounder.
           The Cook caught 2 perch.

Moved under power to the mouth of the northern entrance
to the Babit Lake where after vainly cruising about seeking
shallower water we eventually anchored in seven fathom, a little
way below a raft bridge which made entry of the actual lake
impossible, except for the canoes which slid underneath the
sloping gangway down which carts rattled from the bank to the
raft, or by very little boats which were simply lugged out and
over the raft and re-launched on the other side. The bridge was
fixed in the spring when the ice went and removed before the ice
came. It was never opened in the summer and Racundra had to
be content to lie below it. I should say here that we still believed
that the Babit Lake was what it seemed to be on our map, a huge
sheet of open water, with villages on its banks. We had already
planned which inlets should be our anchorages and it was not
until much later that we learnt its real character. We found the
entrance simply a very deep, broad cut with thickly wooded
banks. On one side there was a little strip of meadow, on the other
the banks rose steeply, great masses had fallen into the water
with the spring floods, and here and there the roots of submerged
pine trees showed on the surface. It was not surprising later to
hear from a member of the Riga yacht club that in trying to
anchor near the shore be had run his ship aground in deep
water, sounding and finding several fathom all round her, her
keel being firmly wedged in the roots or branches of
a submerged tree.

Soon after we had anchored and were getting our fishing tackle
ready we saw a man, a woman and a little dog, with a big bait
can, and a bundle of fishing rods like the fasces of the lictors
walk out on the raft bridge. They settled down one at each end of
the bridge to fish for bait and, as fast as they caught them, set
up, one after another fourteen pike rods in commanding positions
along the bridge and on shore. There was a method, a solemnity
about their procedure that rather withered our own confidence.
What was one pike rod against a forest of them? And indeed we
did very badly. The Cook caught some perch, but I, spinning from
the reel, spinning here, there and everywhere, in deep water, in
shallow close along the shore, in clear water and between the
weeds, with Holroyd Spinners, with spoons, with every different
kind of spinner I possessed, in the course of the whole day had
a run from one very little fish which got off as I was about to
lift him into the boat to release him. Towards evening, when
I saw they were packing up, I paddled up to the bridge to see
what the forest had done. The forests had caught one pike,
a three pounder, and were very pleased with it. But though
I had almost caught the fourteenth part of this, which would
set my rod right as against their multitude, I had learnt that
by spinning I could expect only the most foolish of pike in this

*All day long the regular fishermen
...had gone past us.*

place. All day long the regular fishermen in their canoes had
gone past us up the Babit, over the raft and away into the lake,
and every single boat and canoe dragged a spinner behind it.
Twenty, thirty, forty boats a day went by, and each one with
a spinner, and this during many years. Every pike in the place,
who had not learnt that all is not fish that glitters, had been
caught long ago. Only the numskulls among pike would take such
things, and these had all been caught. The fishermen paddled
along with their spinners towing at the end of a long line. Some
held the line in their teeth. Most had it fastened to one of their
big toes. Now and again we saw them give the line a jerk, but,
watching earnestly, we never saw one of them take a fish. And
watching them returning from the lake I saw their catches, for
the most part eels, rudd and small carp. One man showed me
a pike he had just caught in a trap. One man boasted a pike he
had caught on a spinner but another man called him a liar.
I came to the conclusion that the universal towing of spinners
is a piece of atavism. Once, long ago, pike have been caught by
these means, and human inertia compels the grandsons of the
fortunate fishermen to use their teeth and their big toes in this
way more as a piece of ritual than with any serious hope. I fancied
that I might have had a chance with a blue and silver swallow-
tail of rubber, which, in Russia I found pike took who were long
past paying any attention to spoons and other metal spinners,
but, unfortunately the last of these I had lost some time before.
I ended by writing off spinning for pike here as a bad job.

(Small book)

Entrance to Babit

Thursday Aug 7.

Got our anchor and under the donkey steamed away from St. Johanna, the local population waving handkerchiefs and aprons from among the trees to bid us farewell. Anchored about a hundred yards below the bridge finding seven fathom, a good deal more than we wished, though as near the bank as I thought comfortable. The wind was southwest and we found a sheltered place by waterlilies and fished. The Cook caught two perch. On the banks and the bridge were a family of three, two men and a woman who brought with them fourteen rods and a number of light rods for catching bait. The woman remained on the bridge catching bait. The men moved hurriedly from one pike rod to another. At the end of the day they had caught one three pounder. This was better than I had done. I hooked a little one on float tackle and the Cook seeing it as I brought it towards the boat cried, "Its a very little one" and I tried to lift it straight into the boat with the result that I lost it. In the evening I wriggled my boat through under the end of the raft bridge which lifts sharply to the high bank giving just room to get through lying almost flat and pulling the boat through by tugging at the beams overhead. I caught a perch and a rudd the other side. The senior of the family with the fourteen pike rods told me that the prohibition of fishing in the Babit extends only to the opening of the duck shooting. "I am a lawyer myself and in my opinion they have no right to forbid it, but they get over the difficulty by forbidding boats. They cannot forbid anyone from fishing with rod and line."

Friday 8th August   N. Entrance of Babit.

(Diary)   *Had run from big pike on paternoster.*

Finished Struggle with Private Capital.

Terrific N. wind. Dragged with whole scope of small anchor, dropped great anchor.

Fished near the mouth of the cut and had a run from a pike but failed to hold him. Settled down in the cabin and finished an article. Towards evening the wind shifted and came extremely hard from the north, straight through the cut, with tough rainsqualls. About midnight I felt rather than heard the murmuring grunt and pause of a dragging anchor. It was pitch dark and impossible to see how far we were from the shore. I had the whole scope of our lighter chain down, which in all but the most exceptional occasions is all that we use at sea. There was nothing for it but to put down the great anchor with the heavy chain, a thing of dread, especially when short-handed. I got enough of the heavy chain on deck, lashed the tiller to give the ship a slight sheer to starboard and hauled in as much as I dared on the lighter chain. If I had been able to assure myself that we had not already drifted too far I should have hauled it up altogether and saved much subsequent trouble. Naked, and enjoying the cold douche of these northerly rainsqualls I did not make a very seamanlike job of it, but, making sure that I was not dropping the heavy anchor on the top of the chain from the anchor already out I dropped the monster, veered out a lot of the heavy chain told the elements that they would have a job before them if they meant to shift that and hurried back into the cabin to rub down and still the chattering of my teeth.

(Small book)

Friday. Aug. 8.

Got up at four, tried to go to the Babit but found the water had sunk so low that I could not get my boat through nor could the local fishermen, many of whom turned back, and one man who had gone up to the Babit the night before got stuck at the bridge, and I helped him pull his boat out of the water and over the raft. He had a fine lot of what they call 'carass' in Russian, which I think are carp. While I was fishing just below the raft bridge one of the local fishermen passed me going up. I warned him that he would not be able to get through. "You may not be able" said he, "but I can". I said nothing and watched. He ran his boat into the opening and stuck. His face changed in the most amusing way. Then, obstinate no doubt on account of what he said to me, he took out all his nets and tackle, even the bottom boards of the boat. Even so he could not get through. He loaded all his stuff in again and went off swearing quietly and continuously to himself. In the still early morning I could hear him, swearing still, when he was already

*far away and going out towards the big river. I went, just to
see what would happen and spun between two reed beds just
where my little pike of yesterday had been. He came again,
took my spinner and, as if there were a fate upon me, I lost
him again in exactly the same way, close to the boat. He
dropped in the water and was so surprised that he gave me
time to make a scoop at him with the landing net, but was not
surprised enough not to collect himself in time and dive under
it. That destroyed my morale and I did nothing but miss fish
thereafter. I went to a deep backwater by the opening into the
river, a depth of four fathom or thereabouts and put a big
roach down on a paternoster. It was taken at once by a big
fish, over ten pounds I should judge, who carried it a long way
away and then when I wound in to strike, came straight
towards me so that I could not hit hard with the light seven
foot rod I was using. He threw up the bait and the tooth
marks on it were half an inch deep. This encounter put me in
very good spirits none the less. There really was a big fish
here and at least I had said how do you do to him, and I
rowed back to the ship and settled down to work. I finished
an article for the Guardian and in the evening when the rain
stopped the Cook went off to fish for bait but got nothing but
a bleak and was presently driven in by wind and rain. The
wind came very hard from the northwest and about ten o'clock
I felt that we were dragging. We went out, in the dark. At
least I went on deck dressed in spectacles and a southwester.
'The Royal Nonsuch' said the Cook who had just been reading
Huckleberry Finn. It was very cold and the rain was like ice
water. With great difficulty I put down the heavy anchor but
had to drop it where we lay because we had dragged into eight
fathom and I could not haul in on the light anchor. A most
un-seamanlike job, but the big anchor is so heavy and its chain
is so heavy that the sheer weight of it seemed to give the little
anchor the help it needed and we dragged no more. Got to bed
at one o'clock and slept till seven thirty.*

Saturday August 9th   N. Entrance of Babit.

(Diary)   *Up early caught 5 bait, 1 perch.*

*Fished all day in N. wind like a fool
with the natural result.*

Next day there was still a northerly wind, but fine weather to it and we had another unsuccessful day's fishing. In the evening the Cook announced that there was nothing for it but to move to the nearest market because she had nothing left in the larder.

(Small book)

Saturday. Aug 9.

Got up at seven thirty and went and fished for bait from the raft, and had a very delightful time with the light rod catching five good bait and one perch. The wind was northerly still and strong, so that there was small hope of good fishing and I was foolish to waste the day on it, which I did without result, getting two indecisive runs and no fish. The barometer rose two tenths, but the sky looks extremely stormy. I feel very unhappy because I promised a little boy some roubles for some worms and he got the worms, very good ones, and I found I had no roubles in my pocket and now do not know where to find him.

Sunday August 10th   Scholk.

(Diary) *To Shlok.*

Early in the morning of the tenth, Sunday, I began to recover chain and finally we got the great anchor. It is easy to write that. Remember that we were in seven fathom of water and that we have no windlass or capstan that will take this chain. We hauled it in a few yards at a time, resting reading and smoking between each haul and dreading the actual hoisting of the anchor itself, which, however, came up without the slightest trouble. With the ordinary anchor, it was the other way about. I set the sails. The Cook took the tiller. I ran the chain in hand over hand till it was straight up and down, cast the boat on the port tack and expected to pull the anchor up as if it were a small roach. A few feet of chain came on board with great difficulty and then it was as if I were hauling with it the whole world. I could not shift it an inch. I fixed a double tackle with the spare fore halyards from the top of the mast and lifted it one foot. The Cook added her not inconsiderable weight to mine without making the difference of half an inch. When it

A ruined factory of which a small part is repaired and in working order with one chimney, smoking busily.

dragged it must have caught a tree, or maybe a cannon. We were inclined to think it was a cannon. This place was fortified during the war, and abandoned. There might be anything on the bottom. Whatever it was, it was clear enough that we could not lift it. The only hope that I could see was to slack away a little chain and see what could be done by pulling it sideways along the bottom. So I let out the sheets a little and invited Racundra to take a share in the work while I sat on the forehatch devising a method of applying to an anchor the dodge used in fishing when a spinner gets caught on a snag. I was thinking how to pass a ring down over the anchor chain, fastened to our long coir warp, which I would then take ashore. Suddenly the strain on the tackle somehow looked less. We were moving. Racundra had pulled the anchor clear of the obstruction, cannon or tree. I had the anchor on deck in a moment and in another ten we had tacked out of the cut and were reaching eastwards up the river. The wind was north west and we had easy sailing for a couple of miles with pastoral country to starboard and pine forest to port, until the river bent sharply to the north and we had to tack to and fro between a great expanse of floating logs tethered off a sawmill and on the other side of the river a green island with weedy shallows. It was at this point, of course, that we met a tug with a huge lumber raft, a quarter of a mile or more in length coming down the river. Above the sawmills is a ruined factory of which a small part is repaired and in working order with one chimney, smoking busily while its brethren, broken off like nettles by the sweep of war, may be seen, as stumps beside it. Then, all on the northern bank of the river, is a pier, trees along a road, lampposts, a pompous house with pillars, a restaurant, another pier in ruins, a ferry, horses and carts waiting to cross it, and behind all a tall wooden skeleton tower, today decked out

Scholk: trees along a road and a pompous house with pillars.

with Latvian flags of red and white, the watch-tower of the fire
brigade. This, is Scholk.

Hickory, dickory dock,
Racundra came to Scholk.
She found it was harder
To fill up her larder
By fishing than shopping at Scholk.

We anchored above the ferry beyond the ruined steamer pier and,
as it looked like turning to rain, had the sails down fast and the
covers on them before a fat man in shirt sleeves began bawling
from the shore to the effect that we should be in the way of the
steamer. Unfortunately I believed him and got into the dinghy and
towed Racundra across to the right bank where we anchored again
in two and a half fathoms. We found later that the first berth we
had taken up was the better being well inside the steamer track,
whereas the berth in the southern side, to which we had been
directed was close to the course followed by tugs, hay barges,
lumber rafts and all the miscellaneous traffic of the river.

The rain whose promised coming had hurried us with stowage of
our sails held off, and presently I put mast and sail in the dinghy
and sailed across to the little town, waited in the deafening drunken
row of the wooden restaurant and brought back pork chops, ready
cooked, to the great relief of the Cook. It was Sunday and already
too late for marketing, but I learnt that there would be a market
in the early morning in a little tree-fringed square close to the
river. The evening was calm, and we fished by the reeds, and,
now that we were within reach of stores, learnt by accident the
secret of catching the large perch on which we had expected to
live. We were fishing with worm. The Cook caught a tiny bleak,

and I said, remembering fishing for perch with minnows in my boyhood, "Leave it on for a minute or two and see what happens." She dropped it back in the water and in another minute her float slid under, her reel screamed, and she was playing a stout perch of three quarters of a pound, the first decent fish we had caught.

There was a particularly fine sunset. Racundra in the parting glow of the sun looked almost luminous, the factory chimney stood up like a pillar of fire, and, on the shore behind Racundra were round fiery sheep, a log hut, an ancient boat, and a group of trees in a hundred shades of transparent green. As the sun went down we rowed back to Racundra and, sluicing down the decks, I saw the town of Scholk as a long row of flat cardboard trees, houses and factories, in deep soft blacks and purples on a narrow strip of orange sky.

Monday August 11th   Scholk.

(Diary) *Went to Town.*

(Log)   *Monday 11.*
        Night it rained. Returned to Scholk.
        Fished for perch with small bleak caught by the Cook.
        She caught a good one. I missed two.

Tuesday August 12th   S.W. Entrance of Babit.

(Diary) *Sailed to Babit S.W. entrance.*
        Caught large perch.

(Log)   *Tuesday Aug. 12. Laid in stores at Scholk.*
        Caught bleak.
        Small boys undressing in an old sugar case.
        Bathing under the pier. Running to hide. Sailed at 3.
        Weedy swamp. Through the corner posts.
        Shifted to the bank. Cows. Little houses (farms).
        Anchored in W. entrance to Babit. 4 fathoms.
        Fished. I got 1. Cook missed 5. Swallows over smooth
        water like bands of very fast skaters over clear ice.
        Venus & Mars on opposite sides of the Moon.
        Slight current out of Babit. Fish leaping everywhere.

I had a pleasant bout of sailing in the dinghy in the early morning, and later took the Cook to the largest of the wooden piers. She went into Scholk to buy stores, while I filled the bait can with small bleak, which I caught at the end of the pier, the fish being extraordinarily bold and seemingly not disturbed in the least by the splashing of three small boys who undressed in an upturned packing case and bathed vociferously a few feet from the end of my rod. When the Cook returned, the small boys bolted into their packing case like rabbits into a burrow, and crouched inside it lifting wet and tousled heads, one at a time, to scout over the edge. We sailed at three and, noticing a sawmill with a quay and a barge lying alongside it and another building on shore, all on the left bank of the river, the western bank that is, at a point where the river turns sharply east, and remembering that at these bends of the river we always found deeper water on the outside edge of the bend, we made sure that the channel must be somewhere on the same side as the sawmill. We were mistaken. We came nearer and nearer to the sawmill, nearer and nearer to reedy outposts that seemed to stretch from one side of the river to the other, with seemingly an unbroken line of reeds behind them. We were already getting into shallow water when I gave it up, put the helm down (we were sailing on the port tack with a south-easterly wind) and went across to the eastern shore before turning south again. Keeping near the eastern shore we saw a post sticking up out of the water and steering for it saw another beyond it and then another well away round the corner. We stirred mud in one place with our centreboard, which I thereupon hauled up almost completely. We slid through forests of underwater weeds. In a smooth patch we could see a stony bottom close under our keel. I ceased to wonder why some Riga yachtsmen hold this bend by Pawassern in some respect. The channel is extremely narrow, not deep, and takes two very sharp turns. We wriggled through it and as soon as we were in clear water again, anchored under the right bank of the river, and took stock of the position, with a view of making no mistakes on our way back. Sailing directions for this bend for boats coming up river should be, we decided, as follows. After Scholk keep to the right bank of the river. On the point by the bend, on this same right bank is a small farm. On the shore is a fairly conspicuous tree, which in line with the farm leads to the first spar buoy marking the channel. Approach this buoy very closely, when, if the light is right and the sun not behind them, you will with difficulty be able to make out two posts on land on the opposite side which show beyond the bend. These in line lead close past two more spar buoys. On the left shore on the outer edge of the bend is a cottage, with a post in front of it. A second post at first hidden becomes visible as you approach the second buoy. BEFORE these two are in line you must begin to turn and as soon as they are in line they will lead you clear into deep water beyond the bend.

A big tarred boat high and dry on shore.

If you hold on too long on the line of the first pair you are in shallow water before you get the second pair in line. Reverse these directions coming down the river. Once you know what to look for there is really no difficulty, but the posts on land are difficult to see and as there are no charts of the river the newcomer does not know where to begin looking.

When we had settled these points and eaten a large tea, we got the anchor up and tacked on past two or three little farms in the trees, each one with a big tarred boat high and dry on shore, a relic of a time when there must have been considerable sailing traffic on the river. At Gate the river bends again and we were able to reach comfortably past the farms of Kaling and Selme Oding, watching the reeds for the southwestern entrance to the Babit. This entrance runs east and west, and when we found it we were able to sail close hauled directly into it. The land on either side was bare swamp, and we had no fear here of catching trees or cannon with our anchor. The lead gave us a steady four fathom, and, as soon as we thought we were far enough in to be free from the wash of the steamers in the river, and near a little opening in the reeds and a patch of waterlilies that seemed to promise fish, we rounded up to the wind and anchored for the night. As soon as we had put the covers on the sails we brought the dinghy alongside, loaded it with fishing rods and anchored it close by the patch of waterlilies. We fished for perch with small bleak as bait. I got one. The Cook had five runs, the fish in each case taking out a lot of line and in each case escaping unhooked. We came to the conclusion that it must be a small pike who was grabbing the bait just for practice, but, not being hungry was not turning it ready to swallow, but was just swimming about with it across his jaws as I have sometimes seen them in clear water. The wind had dropped to nothing as we put the anchor down. The evening was perfectly calm, everywhere fish were rising to flies, and great crowds of swallows pursued them over the smooth water, all rushing together up the narrow cut, in little crowds, like bands of very fast skaters over clear ice. As it grew dark I smoked in the cockpit, watching a red star and a white, Mars and Venus, perhaps, on opposite sides of the Moon.

Wednesday August 13th   Kalnzeem under motor.

(Diary) *Caught a fine lot of big perch.*
Sailed to Kalnzeem under sail & motor.

(Log) *Wed. Aug 13. Up at 4. Nothing. Between 11 & 2*
caught many fine perch. Up to 1 pound.
Started under power at 3.45.
Hoisted mainsail. Anchored at 6 at Kalnzeem.

Perch are the most capricious fish. I got up on their behalf at four in the morning and fished in one good-looking place after another until the foghorn called me to breakfast on Racundra. I did not have a single bite. Yet after breakfast, as the Cook was not ready to start, I took the dinghy out again, and between eleven and two o'clock caught a magnificent lot of them, hardly a fish under the half pound and the best of them well over a pound.

At 3.45 we started away under power. There was a slight wind to keep our sails full but no more, when standing close hauled, so I hoisted the mainsail, which slightly improved our pace. Both shores were fringed with a belt of tall reeds. Far away over the marshes to the west we could see a line of thick forest. To the east were a few stony hillocks with scattered, worried-looking pines on them, where the old German front had been during the war. On either side of the river behind the reeds was flat swampland, with here and there a small farm. Before we reached Kalnzeem we passed an opening on the right bank of the river, the lower end of a channel that divides a long very narrow island from the mainland. We met a small copy of Racundra, built this year in Riga, but a poor thing, and top heavy (I heard afterwards that she would stand no wind, and that in anything more than a light breeze she became unmanageable, at which I was not surprised). At Kalnzeem we found a bunch of houses, a ferry, and a steamer pier, and decided we could do no better than stop here. We anchored close by the

Hardly a fish under the half pound.

head of the island, where we could see into a most tempting little channel of smooth water, completely sheltered by high reeds and small trees, a perfect place for fish as we thought. I hoisted the sail in the dinghy and sailed away up river, tacking slowly against the slight breeze and landed by the ferry. No one seemed willing to sell me any milk. I went from one house to another and came finally to the schoolhouse, where I found a schoolmaster very surly at

Stony hillocks with scattered, worried looking pines on them.

*A channel of smooth water,
completely sheltered by high reeds.*

being interrupted from the reading of his newspaper. He told me
he had no milk. Just then his wife came in, as stout as he was
meagre, and declared that she had some milk that I may have.
She got the milk, and I offered a Lat (fifty roubles, a little less
than a shilling). She had no change and was going to take the milk
away again, when the schoolmaster intervened and told her that as
she had wanted to let me have milk when he had already told me
there was none she must jolly well, (or words to that effect) go and
get change, which she did very sulkily. They were not a happy pair.
Their milk however was excellent.

Thursday August 14th   Motor and sail to Wolgund.

(Diary) *Kalnzeem to Wolgund. Motor sail.*

The She Apothecary.

Stork in chimney which was damaged during the war.

Eclipse of moon.

Rows of little factories, with little left standing but the chimneys.

(Small book)

The Apothecary at Wolgund.

Started under motor from Kalnzeem but had strong headwind and the little donkey could make nothing of it, so I hoisted first main and then mizzen and tacked up the river keeping the motor going. In the shallow bend at Umul we found ourselves among weeds, and the centreboard stirred up the mud a little. I shall have to dive again and clean our propeller of weeds. Along the left bank of the river there was a long row of little factories, little left standing but the chimneys, a desolate sight. But it was weary disheartening work tacking away against the wind and current, and the hammering of the little donkey became unbearable. It simply would not be forgotten and I wanted to duck it for a scold.

Our progress was terribly slow. I measured the ground made by the haystacks on the right bank of the river, and was often not sure, since they were all alike, whether we had made any ground or not. One haystack had a fork in the top of it and this became a grateful landmark. We had meant to stop by a narrow inlet at Rudyl, by some ruined factories, but as we got there we got a little present from the wind, and could not but make use of it, as it took us on one board down a stretch of the river and along another. Hereafter the river turned sharp into the wind again, so with a thankful heart (not that I was not very pleased with the little beast) I shut off the motor, and cruised to and fro under main and mizzen along this last

Haystacks on the right bank of the river.

stretch and anchored between a factory chimney with the top knocked off and a curious brick and oak beamed house that might have been transplanted from Stratford on Avon. Beside this house was a fine plantation of trees and among the trees a broken down mansion. Looking at Shakespeare's house through the glasses I saw that it was an apothecary's shop. That was one point of interest about it, here far from anywhere was not a general store, or a blacksmith's but a chemist's, it struck me as odd. Another point of interest was a huge erection of twigs on one end of the roof, shaped like but completely dwarfing the chimneys. I thought it was a stork's nest but was not sure. So, taking the excuse of getting milk, I cast off the dinghy and went ashore.

(Notes. Small Book)

Mrs. Apothecary. Milk.

She and I go for a walk round estate.

Her trade better in winter than in summer.

The storks (she thought I was interested in swallows).

Why does England buy butter?

The Germans in the chimney on other side of the river.

The damage done by the Bermondtski.

The carp pond.

The break up of the estate.

The little houses all new. Sprung up in the waste left by the war. A few whose houses unfinished still living in the ruined mansion. The big trees and garden seats. Dances every other Sunday when drunkards throw their bottles into the carp pond. Small boys get little carp in baskets but her son met a big carp when swimming.

Sailing at night. The stork on the top of the chimney watching eclipse of the moon.

The door of the house was open.

Wolgund

The door of the house was open, I walked in and found a small room with a counter and some large stone jars on shelves behind it. A little girl looked mouse like at me round a corner and disappeared, and presently the apothecary, a stout, thoroughly humane woman in a purple blouse came in. In a few moments she had put me through a fire of questions, as if I was a patient, and she about to prescribe. She had learnt my nationality, the name of my boat, the size of my boat, the fact that I was married, the destination of my boat, where we had spent the previous night, the cost of building such a boat, and the fact (which she did not believe) that we had nothing to sell on board. She gulped the answers whole to these questions one after another in a single rush, like a pike coming through and depleting a shoal of bleak. Only the last answer seemed to stick. That she could not swallow. She was convinced that we had a cargo of strange merchandise that we were reserving for sale higher up the river. At one point in her questioning (I think when she was taking breath) I told her we wanted to buy milk, and, practical woman, she called through the open doorway without pausing to breathe, and told me that in an hour the men will fetch milk. A quart set aside for me.

She had come outside the house during her fire of questions, to see with her own eyes the little ship lying innocently at anchor in the river below her. I made her come a little further and pointed up to the great mass of twigs about the chimney on the top of the house. Was it a nest? So ordinary did the storks seem to her, that she thought I was speaking of the swallow's nest under the eaves. Then she told me that there was a family of young storks in the nest, and that presently the older ones would be coming to take up their place on the top of the factory chimney that rose out of the river and weeds in ruins on the other side of the river. The chimney she said had had its top broken off in the war. It had been a general observation post. One day the Russians began to shell it. Three officers were in it. For half an hour the shells flew by it harmlessly. One of the officers was going down a ladder they had inside it, and was only a little way down when a shell knocked off the top of the chimney and his friends with it.

"Was much damage done by the war?" I asked. "Not so much due to the war, but afterwards the Bermondt anti-Bolshevik troops robbed all they could, and destroyed what they could not carry away. It was they who sacked and looted the old castle of the governor at Mitau."

"And who is living now in that house in the trees?" I asked.

"That was the house of the Wolgund Estate," she said. "But the estate has been divided up, and the people are building themselves little houses each on his own land."

She pointed out the flat country and here and there I could see little new wooden houses, the new wood gleaming in the evening sunlight.

"Those whose houses are not yet done are living in the big house. But stay a moment," she said, and hurried back into her own house, returning with a fine coloured handkerchief on her head.

She then took me for a walk round the garden of the old house in the trees. The house had lost much of the glass from its windows. I suppose the builders of the little new houses needed glass, and took what

...the great mass of twigs about the chimney...

An Arthur Ransome Cruising Classic
(by the author of Swallows & Amazons)

RACUNDRA'S FIRST CRUISE
ISBN 1 898660 96 1
Introduced and compiled by Brian Hammett
Published by Fernhurst Books

Eighty years after its first appearance, Fernhurst Books are publishing a new edition of this famous book. Included in this unique edition are the original maps, text and photographs of the 1923 first edition of Racundra's First Cruise.

Brian Hammett has compiled and introduced this unique edition of *Racundra's First Cruise*. The introduction leads us into a treasure trove of unpublished writings, essays and photographs. Ransome's first attempts at Baltic sailing, in his two previous boats *Slug and Kittiwake*, are explained in detail using his writings and illustrations. The life of Ransome's beloved *Racundra* is chronicled to its conclusion and there is an explanation of how he came to write the book. The original illustrations are enhanced by the inclusion of present day photographs of the same locations.

The book's first edition only ran to 1500 copies, was reprinted many times in various editions and formats but never as the original publication. Ransome's attitude to sailing is summed up in the opening paragraph of *Racundra's First Cruise*:

"Houses are but badly built boats so firmly aground that you cannot think of moving them. They are definitely inferior things, belonging to the vegetable not the animal world, rooted and stationary, incapable of gay transition. I admit, doubtfully, as exceptions, snail-shells and caravans. The desire to build a house is the tired wish of a man content thenceforward with a single anchorage. The desire to build a boat is the desire of youth, unwilling yet to accept the idea of a final resting-place."

Brian Hammett, who received critical acclaim for his work on *Racundra's Third Cruise*, (published by Fernhurst in spring 2002) has produced another excellent book.

The book will delight cruising yachtsmen, sailing historians and Ransome's fans everywhere.

ORDER FORM

Available from bookshops, chandlers, direct from the Editor, or from Fernhurst Books

To Brian Hammett, Wren's Park, Chelmsford Road, Blackmore, Essex. CM4 0SG.

☎ +44(0)1277 821481 e-mail wrenspark@aol.com

Please send me, post free, ...copies of Racundra's First Cruise at £20.00 each

I enclose cheque/postal order payable to Brian Hammett for £ ....

Name.. Address..

....

....

...factory chimney... in ruins on the other side of the river.

they wanted, while those camped in the big house boarded up the gaping windows. A lovely place it must have been with huge old trees and garden seats arranged with secret pictures of the river through the trees.

Then she, the apothecary, and I walked all round the house and came to a fine artificial pond, with a lawn behind it trodden into mud, with the trappings of secret trysts scattered on it, and a rough bandstand at one side and bushes round it.

"Here," she said, "They dance every other Sunday. It is a pity you could not be here for that."

She evidently saw herself and me solemnly caracoling under the trees. I asked if there were fish in the pond.

"There are carp. The children catch little ones in baskets. My son met a big one when he was swimming to the middle. But now no one swims in it, for after the dancing those who drink too heavily throw their bottles into the pond and the bottom, or so my son says, is covered with broken glass."

A question that had evidently bothered her for some time came suddenly into her mind.

"England is a rich country," she said.

"More or less" said I, wondering what she was after.

"Then why do they need our butter?"

"Because we have not enough of our own."

…I could see little new wooden houses…

*"But if it is a rich country I suppose everybody has plenty
of land of his own. Why do they not keep cows?"*

*I tried to explain, but she had it firmly in her head that the English
were a rich but lazy race, and preferred to buy butter from abroad
rather than be bothered with cows. I asked her about her own work.*

*"My husband was a doctor," she said. "But he is in Russia and
I daresay he is dead. I remember well enough what he did and
when people are ill they come to me and I have always something
to do them some good. But summer is a bad time for us, what with
the steamer, anyone who is ill can go to Mitau in a steamer so they
do not come to us. But in winter when the river is frozen, why then
they can only get to Mitau skating and so I do good business.
Because more people are ill in winter."*

*On the whole she did pretty well, and indeed a woman so
practical and insatiable of knowledge could hardly fail to do
well anywhere. I thought of feigning illness and having her
prescribe for me. But that would have lowered to the professional
plane the whole tone of our intercourse, which was genial,
humane, and spacious as between citizens of the world.*

*We strolled together under the old trees until my milk was ready,
when we parted with expressions of mutual respect, though in her
last sentence, speaking of the good inhabitants of Mitau, she was
not above a delicate hint that we were a little unkind in reserving
our cargo for the more fortunate citizens of the town.*

I put the milk on board and then hoisting my sail cruised up and down in the dusk. The stork came and sailed round overhead, perching at last on the top of the broken factory chimney. The moon shone out, and while I watched it, changed its shape.

We had seen no newspapers for some days, and did not know that at that moment people were crowding the streets of Riga and the roofs of the houses to observe an eclipse of the moon. Wolgund knew nothing about it and missed it. The eclipse in these parts was watched by the crew of Racundra, and the stork who, standing erect on his chimney, now and then lifted his wing, as if a little troubled in his mind and needing to fly, but always thought better of it, closing his wing again, and now and then thinking that the moon might change its habit if it wished but it could not be.

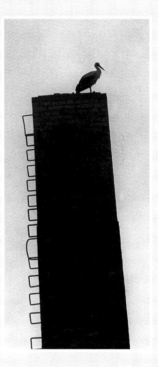

The stork...
standing erect on his chimney...

Friday August 15th   Ekau River & Mitau ditch.

(Diary)   *Sailed Wolgund to Ekau river mouth against hard S.E. wind.*

Saw marsh harrier & more storks.
Went up Ekau river in dinghy. Caught few perch.

Evening under power up to steamer ditch to Mitau. Jews. Rowing Club. Escaped in the moonlight back to Ekau river. Our main lubricator cracked.

While sluicing down the decks in the early morning I saw a marsh
harrier, that most unmistakeable of hawks, with his buff cap,
swinging low above the reeds close to us. Once or twice he dropped
into the reeds but I could not see what he got there. Each time
he stopped he remained hidden for a full half minute, so maybe
he was after very small game, such as dragonflies, which he ate
before rising again.

The wind was southeasterly, against us, but by breakfast time
there was plenty of it and as we had promised to be in Mitau by
Saturday I decided to push on and save paraffin. The stork had left
the tall chimney but did not go to the great nest on the roof of the
female apothecary's house. He was evidentially worried about us,
and not accustomed to seeing a stout seagoing ketch anchored so
close under his riverside bungalow. Our rig was probably strange
to him who was more familiar with Arab dhows and huge lateen
sails. He flew slowly to and fro across the river, nearer and nearer
to us, as if making up his mind to perch on our masthead. Perhaps
he took our burgee on its slender flagstaff as some strange cousin
of his own, also given to roosting on one leg. He did not leave us
till we had rounded the corner by Laukgal and were heading south
and making the most of a stretch on which the wind was a little
more favourable.

It was fairly hard work for Racundra beating up the narrow river
and we had one or two anxious moments, particularly at Plerren
where there was once a bridge, the remains of which, submerged
all but the broken girder ends just above water, leave none too
much room for a vessel beating through against the wind, and, as
there are no charts of the river, we had no means of knowing what
else there might be under water besides the just visible remains
of the piers. However we got through all right and, resisting the
temptation to stop and fish in one or two most promising little
reedy creeks, we fought out and tacked up to the mouth of the
Ekau River. Here according to our map the low end of an island
divides the Aa into two individual streams. The head of the island
is actually in Mitau and we had not out the slightest idea which of
the two channels we should take. I anchored accordingly out of the
channel on the eastern side to wait until observation of passing
steamers should enable me to filch a little 'local knowledge'.

Just as the anchor went down a small roughly built canoe with a
tiny square sail came down the river with a fine bubble of water
under her prow, flew past Racundra within a few feet of her and
luffing suddenly shot, as the squaresail came down, through
a tiny gap in the reeds into the Ekau river. The sight of this local
fisherman, for I had seen a bundle of rods in his boat, was too
much for me. I had seen as we passed the mouth that there was

High reeds and bushes sheltered the little river completely.

smooth sheltered water in the Ekau River, whereas there were
white tops to the waves in the Aa. I took my rods, dropped into the
dinghy and made for the gap where the canoe had disappeared.
Going through those reeds was like coming out of a tunnel in a
train, a sudden transition from tumult to silence. The wind was
blowing straight down the Aa but across the Ekau, and the high
reeds and bushes sheltered the little river completely. I rowed up
it in great satisfaction, found a large pool with trees above it close
below the bridge, and presently missed a small pike, and made up
for it by catching a snag of some kind and losing my spinner. This
was the last spinner I had with me, so I settled down to fish for
perch, but got only a few and they much smaller than those I had
had in the entrance to the Babit. I was presently content to do
nothing, and watch a small boy fishing very skilfully with a long
straight branch of willow I think, peeled and white. Now and again
he caught a little fish. I tried to talk to him but we could find no
language known to us both, or perhaps he was a born fisherman.

When I returned to Racundra for tea, I found the wind dropping.
I saw a tug come down the eastern branch of the river but two
steamers from Riga went up the western branch, so we decided to
do the same. It was altogether too narrow for tacking and the little
donkey could not have forced us against the wind that had held all
day. But at seven the wind was much less and getting the anchor
up we steamed round the low end of the island and up the western
branch. It was very narrow and the further we went up the more
doubtful we became. Narrow as it was, the channel in it was still
narrower. The Cook steered, while on the foredeck I watched for the
masses of weeds that must be avoided by our propeller. Over the

I returned to Racunda for tea.

low land before us we could see the churches of Mitau, and at
the head of the island a low red ruin in trees, which we learnt
afterward was the old castle of the Governor. Here and there
at the sides of our ditch, for it was no more, men were fishing
in flat-bottomed boats. The wind died altogether, and only the
continual rising of fish broke the water. The ditch narrowed until
there was not room for Racundra to turn round. There was nothing
for it but to go on. The green swamps ended. There were little
tumbledown wooden houses to starboard, with a stretch of mud in
front of them, and piles driven in the edge of the ditch. Children
were bathing in the muddy water. We had made up our minds to
turn in a fine blue blob on our map, but when we came to it we
found that the blue only meant that it was not land and did not
mean that it was water. It was nothing but a reedy swamp. We slid
on into the town. We passed a barge and then another tied to posts
on the western bank under the houses.

A young Jew and his father were superintending the loading of
one of the barges. I shouted to him to know if there was better
anchorage further up. He was immensely anxious that we should
anchor where we were.

"Here, here," he shouted. "Anchor here. Here is the best place.
By those posts. Lay her alongside the posts. Deep water. Steamers
used to berth there. Where you come from? Do you do it for
pleasure? Have you been on the sea? Is it not dangerous in
storms? No. No. Nearer to us."

He poured out words as if he were a rotary word pump and became terribly excited at the thought that we might go further up the ditch and be lost to him. We were a social event of great magnitude. He wanted us all to himself, not for our good but for his own. "Here. Here," he cried. "Here you have company."

Fortunately I did not entirely trust him, but stopping Racundra and anchoring in mid-ditch, dropped into the dinghy and took a stern line that I had already made fast on board to one of the posts alongside which he urged that we should moor. The depth by the posts was under two feet. I grieve to say that I shook my fist at that young Jew. I made fast temporarily, and left Racundra so in midstream while I rowed another hundred yards up the ditch looking for a better anchorage. The ditch disappeared under a bridge. On this side of the bridge there was the steamer quay, with an open space before it just giving room for the steamer to be warped round. Opposite was a rowing club. The depth of water by their pier was not more than a couple of feet. The position was hopeless. I asked one of the rowing club people, who was lounging about in a gorgeous yachting costume if he could tell me where I should have anchored for the night, and where yachts usually anchored. Like the young Jew he was delighted at our arrival, determined to possess us as a social event, and completely careless as to whether we liked the arrangement or not. He began to get ready a little motor dinghy, and called excitedly to his friends that a strange yacht had come and that he would take them to see it.

I looked at the sky. The sun had set. It was already nearly dark. But there was going to be a moon. The stink of the ditch was overpowering. I spun the dinghy round and rowed back to Racundra. I calculated that we should just be able to turn her. Casting loose the stern rope, I took it round the post and back on board, so that the Cook could release it at the right moment. Then I got the donkey going. I fixed a towrope to the dinghy, and got the anchor up and down. At this moment the decorative yachtsman arrived in his motor boat and so far from offering us a tow wedged himself between the dinghy and Racundra, got tangled in the towrope extricated himself from that and laid himself across the bows of the dinghy so that I could not pull, all the time trying to impress his associates with his own knowledge of foreign languages. Choosing our moment, the Cook cleverly swung the anchor off the ground. I pulled for all I was worth. Racundra's head came round. The Cook let go the stern rope and hauled it on board, a mass of mud and slime. I got a little way on Racundra, and then clambering on board pulled over the lever that puts the propeller in action. We were off. If we should run aground on the way out even that would be better than remaining in an open drain to be bumped on hard bottom by each steamer that should pass. It was very dark, but with what moon there was we could just catch the glint of the water. The Cook steered. I conned from the foredeck and between us we brought her back by the way we had come, touching nowhere, and turning round the low end of the island anchored as nearly as we could where we had been anchored in the afternoon. We took delighted breaths of the clean air, had a late supper and turned in.

Saturday August 16th   Mitau.

(Diary)   *5 a.m. under power up Aa river to Mitau.*

Anchored in 5 fathom by the bridge.
Wrote 4 pp. Com. Party rank & file.

Lunched on shore.

Sailed in dinghy up to railway bridge.

(Handwritten notes)

Mitau Jelgrava

Ruined palace among the trees. Burnt out palace without a pane of glass like that in the story of the Soldier and Death, where no one could live because of the devils. A ruddy terracotta building standing gauntly among the green trees.

Market square. On the end of a building is painted a huge picture of a galloping tiger, a tiger of a child's imagination, galloping over a lilac dessert, with conical mountains in a muddy background. Nothing is missing except the sun. And in one of Mitau's bombardments, a lucky shell hit the apex of the roof exactly at the top of the picture, and burst there, fragments of shell cutting through to the brick, in downward slanting rays and the splash of the shell itself enriching the galloping tiger with a sun as heraldic as himself.

In the evening we were hailed from the shore by a boy with a telegram addressed 'Yacht Racundra, Mitau, River Aa'. It was to say that our guest was not coming but it left us rather elated. We felt it was to Racundra's credit that she should be a successful telegraphic address.

Ancient trees and behind them the long red palace.

At five in the morning, while the Cook slept, I started the little donkey, got the anchor up, and steamed against a very slight wind up the eastern branch of the river to Mitau. The rising sun shone on a little farm with white-leaved willow trees on the island and, as we came nearer to Mitau, lit up the ruddy terracotta ruins of the castle among the green trees. The eastern bank was absolutely bare. We passed first one and then another wooden enclosure for swimming, a little wooden clubhouse with a sailing dinghy tied under it and then before us was a wooden bridge across the river, and we were slipping slowly towards it under a steep green bank, with a terrace, painted seats, orderly ancient trees and behind them the long red palace, a palace without a pane of glass in any of the windows, like that in the story of the Soldier and Death, where no one could live because of the devils. The bridge had also suffered. One pier had gone, and instead there were three lighters as pontoons, supporting a section of bridge much lower than the rest, so that carts rattled down a sleep slope to it and up on the other side. There were houses on each side of the bridge, and close under it on the western side was a little inlet and a tug. Under the palace was a little wooden pier. I decided that the best place to anchor would be below the pontoons, as nothing coming down the river would be able to get through them, so that we should be out of the way of tugs and timber rafts. I stopped the donkey and anchored in four fathoms. The Cook came sleepily on deck and said that we had done well. Thus encouraged, I went marketing.

I made fast the dinghy to the tug, by kind invitation, and walked

The palace was built in the time of Catherine the Great.

through a garden under the gutted palace, a garden with a bronze plaque on a post below the level of the stomach, to say that it had been largely created by the voluntary labour of peasants of the surrounding district. There are many degrees in the quality of good will, and the relations between peasants and their German and Russian employers before the war were not such as to make it possible to believe that the 'voluntary labour' was contributed with any great enthusiasm. I asked someone afterwards precisely what it meant, and was told 'voluntary' means that they did not pay money for the work. It does not mean that they got it for nothing. I dare say that a good many sticks were worn out in the process.

Garden and palace are on the head of the island and there are remains of a moat, and suggestions of a fortified place here long before the building of the palace. The palace was built in the time of Catherine the Great, and finished in 1772. It was begun in 1738 on the site of the old castle, which the Russians had destroyed when they took the town in 1706, and was sacked and gutted by the anti-Bolshevik troops of the fanatic Bermondt, who made himself a black uniform, called himself the Avenger, took no prisoners and supported himself and his troops by wholesale pillage.

Beyond the garden a wooden bridge crosses the smelly ditch from which we had escaped the night before. Two little passenger steamers were moored alongside the quay and I was glad that we had not waited for them. In the main river on the other side we

A huge picture of a galloping tiger.

had plenty of room, and clean air, whereas it was obvious that this ditch served as the town drain. The road over the bridge leads directly into the main square of Mitau. Directly opposite it in the square is the end of a house which some time before the war was a fur-store. On the blank, windowless wall, is painted in pale fresco a huge picture of a galloping tiger, the tiger of a child's nightmare, galloping over a lilac desert with pale mountains in a lavender background. The picture lacked nothing but the sun. And in one of Mitau's many bombardments, in 1918 or 1919, a lucky shell hit the apex of the roof exactly at the top of the picture, and burst there as if on purpose, fragments of shell cutting through the paint to the red brick below it in downward slanting rays, the splash of the shell itself enriching the galloping tiger with a sun as heraldic as himself.

The streets were full of people and the noise of trumpets and drums. It was the birthday of one of the local regiments and troops were marching through the streets carrying before them huge Lettish flags, the red with a white stripe, that was chosen in a hurry before it was realised that it was identical with the Austrian ensign. The white stripe was narrowed by way of marking a distinction. Troops, no doubt the birthday regiment, were parading through the streets. Officers and soldiers of other regiments hurried along the pavements beside them, and all the shopkeepers of Mitau ran out of their shops to see. Even the market was momentarily paralysed by the excitement.

It was a jolly market, of the old fashioned kind, without the

It was a jolly market.

specialisation that has made modern markets more like streets
of shops. There were a few booths, butcher's and baker's and
the sellers of rush baskets, wooden toys, and simple wooden
instruments, spoons, bowls and nutmeg graters. I bought a
magnificent nutmeg grater, and a fine rush basket, still green, to
carry my purchases. But for the most part the market people
had no booths, and transacted their business sitting among the
vegetables in their carts. They had driven in in the early morning,
each cart with its potatoes and cabbages and apples, each cart with
its big can of milk, most of them with a selection of flowers for
sale, some with chickens and ducks, others with eggs, and many
with big wooden trays of little conical sour cream cheeses dusted
over with caraway seeds. You could buy everything everywhere,
and you walked among the carts letting the spirit guide you as
to which would have the best milk and the smallest proportion
of rotten apples among the good. I chose a clean and stout old
lady as being the most likeliest looking of the crowd, and plumped
for her, not distributing my custom, but buying from her eggs,
milk, cream cheeses, butter, apples and a couple of cauliflowers.
Paraffin for the donkey I got at a pleasant shop, which also
supplied tobacco, matches and candles. I staggered back to the
dinghy, and took my load on board.

During the last two days we had noticed that the oil in the
lubricator disappeared much quicker than it should, and that
the base of the engine was dripping with it. We thought that the
lubricator glass was cracked, and I hunted through Mitau to find
another but fortunately failed. During the afternoon I removed

the lubricator and took it to pieces and found that nothing was wrong with it except that the packing was worn out. I made fresh washers with asbestos for lack of leather, and, was delighted with this new stage of intimacy with the one time alien little donkey. My friendship with the little creature progresses almost dangerously and I begin to fear for my old age, that when I am too stiff to handle ropes, I may strike up a disgraceful liaison with a motor boat.

We lunched on shore in a little wooden restaurant under the trees in the garden under the gutted castle. Ices were advertised but there were none. Instead we had some excellent smoked eel and a local cherry brandy. After that we took the dinghy back to Racundra to get the mast and sail, and had a good gusty wind, just the wind to make dinghy sailing a delight, while we went up river under the wooden bridge, past little cottages with fishing nets drying, and under the great railway bridge, and so through to a fine reach of the river which made us regret that Racundra's mast was not in a tabernacle, so that we could lower it, take her above bridges and explore the higher reaches of the river. We sailed back in time for a late tea about the time we expected the train from Riga that should have brought a friend to spend the week end with us. We were smoking in the cockpit when a boy hailed us from the steamer pier with a telegram addressed to "Yacht Racundra, Mitau, River Aa". It was to say that our guest was not coming but it left us rather elated. We felt it was to Racundra's credit that she should be, even so far inland, a successful telegraphic address.

Sunday August 17th   Mitau.

(Diary) *Up at 7.30. Milk from market above bridge.*

Swimming festival.

(Handwritten notes)

On Sunday we found ourselves imprisoned. A barrier of logs was drawn across the river to enclose, quite unnecessarily, the Mitau swimming festival. The banks of the river were crowded with spectators but the majority could see little more than us, and could see a young man in a yachting costume with a megaphone perched on the top of the diving board bending in all directions with his comic instrument and using it so often that he seemed to be making a continuous speech. It was his day, and he was making the most of it, with all Mitau to watch him, though,

in spite of his megaphone they could not hear what he said.
The local sportsmen arrived, preceded by a brass band and
a Lettish banner. Rowing boats with a Lettish yacht ensign
passed by, and a fat youth in an outrigger skiff slid about like
a water spider. The boats jammed together to watch the
swimming could see the young men and women of Mitau one
by one stand on the top of the diving platform with outstretched
arms like sun worshippers and one by one disappear behind the
scaffolding which hid their entry into the water but was not high
enough to hide the more decisive splashes.

On Sunday we rose late and found ourselves imprisoned. A barrier
of logs had been drawn across the river a couple of hundred yards
below us to enclose, quite unnecessarily, the Mitau swimming
festival. Presently the local sportsmen arrived, preceded by a brass
band and a Lettish banner, swelling out their chests and strutting
like gamecocks along the terrace by the castle towards the
swimming baths on the riverside. Rowing boats with the Lettish
yacht ensign passed by and a fat youth in an outrigger skiff,
dressed as for a boatrace, slid about like a water spider doing his
best to attract to himself the attention of those who had come to
see the swimming. The banks were crowded with spectators, and
the boats jammed together along the barrier. From where we lay
we could not see the swimming but we had a fine view of the
central figure of the performance, a young man in a yachting
costume with a megaphone perched on the top of a diving platform,
bending in all directions with his comic instrument and using it so
often that he seemed to be making a continuous speech. It was his
day, and he was making the most of it, with all Mitau to watch
him, though, in spite of his megaphone they could not hear what
he said. Perhaps because of his megaphone they could not hear
him, for we noticed that when he had something really urgent to
say he laid the instrument aside and shouted so to speak with the
naked voice. He was however displaced when the diving competition
began, but, unable to breathe the ordinary atmosphere after his
experience of life on the altitude of the diving platform, he
presently climbed up again, and standing on a ladder a little way
below the divers did his best to vie with the young men and women
who without the advantage of a megaphone, posed one by one
on the platform above his head, stretched up their arms like sun
worshippers, lingered in worship as long as they dared brave the
public opinion of those who were waiting their turns to shine, and
then dropped below the scaffolding which hid from us their actual
entry into the water but was not high enough to hide the more
decisive splashes.

A long stretch of little ruined factories.

Monday August 18th   Kalnzeem.

(Diary) *Sailed with wind hard to Kalnzeem.*
        When anchored & moored to little trees
        lost knife overboard.

        (Got it by diving the next day.)

        Posted 2 articles on Com. Party & Journalism.

We had a good southwesterly wind and after waiting to get fresh
milk, had a fine sail down the river to Kalnzeem. There was indeed
so much wind that it was not easy work photographing, and we
wanted to get photographs of the long stretch of little ruined
factories of the river on the stretch between Dirbe and Grasche.
Nothing could give a more vivid impression of the disaster that
the wars have been to this country. Factory after factory in ruins.
Chimneys in long rows without smoke, in many cases the chimney
alone surviving like a memorial obelisk rising out of a tumulus
made of a wrecked factory. In one place close beside the remains of
a factory we saw a fine house in the rich Russian merchant style,
decorated with a portico and pillars, with a date on it, 1914, and
scarcely a pane of glass left in it, no doubt finished just before the

A tiny little island in the mouth of the canal.

war and wrecked within three years when the Russians, remembering the way they beat Napoleon a hundred years before, destroyed as they retreated. The buildings that survived these operations were ruined in the later struggle to eject from the country the German general Von der Goltz who had lingered here on Churchill's invitation, and the brigand chief Bermondt on whom also at one time were set the hopes of people who did not care what became of the Letts but were ready to support any scoundrel who described himself as anti-Bolshevik.

We came down haystack reach in a very different manner from that in which we had struggled up it. It seemed only a minute or two before we were passing the little clump of buildings at Kalnzeem, when we hugged the right bank of the river and presently rounded to and anchored just in the mouth of the narrow sheltered canal that runs between the island and the mainland. We had admired this place on our way up the river and decided to spend a night in it if possible and see if it was as good for fishing as it looked. I tumbled over into the dinghy and rowed in between willows and reeds, sounding as I went and finding ample depth. There are really two islands here. There is the long island, and, just at this end of it there is another tiny little island in the mouth of the canal, dividing it in two. I decided to bring Racundra in here and tie up behind this little island. I did not want to use the engine because although deep enough it was extremely weedy and I did not want to turn our propeller again into a revolving haystack. So I towed while the Cook steered, and, the wind having shifted to the southeast, had the hardest struggle to move Racundra against it fast enough to prevent her being blown ashore, sheltered as we were. There were only fifty or sixty yards to tow, but I had had more than enough when at last we dropped the anchor near the weather shore and took out stern warps which I made fast round a couple of obliging willows which had obviously grown up for the especial purpose of being bollards for Racundra on the opposite bank. I made all fast and then proceeded to put the covers on the sails and take the staysail off her. In unshackling the staysail I lost my knife overboard, the second misfortune of this kind. I had begun by losing my spectacles off St. Johanna, when I recovered them with the grapnel. This time I took my clothes off and dived but the water was rather thick and I could not find the knife and came up half full of water and persuaded that I had lost it for good.

I had brought Racundra in here solely because it looked an inviting little place where we should be out of the way of all traffic and possibly catch fish. It had never occurred to me that we should be glad of this shelter for another reason. But when I went below after tidying up, I saw that the barometer had dropped like a thunderbolt. The wind got up in squalls shifting continually, and soon after dark we were thanking our stars that we were where we were. We should have had to pay out chain at the anchorage outside and that would have brought us into the steamer channel, which at this point is very narrow. Flash after flash of lightning, with resounding claps of thunder almost simultaneous with the flashes, lit the little canal so that we could see every reed as if in sunlight. The flashes were almost continuous and the friendly little haven was no longer a pleasant leafy green shelter but a curious livid unearthly place. We had hail on deck and rain that churned up the water and ran from our scuppers with the noise of small streams. However the decks had taken up well, and the cabin was dry enough. We stayed in it, playing bezique by the light of the cabin lamp, which now and again was turned pale when a more than usually brilliant flash lit up the cabin as if at midday.

Tuesday August 19th   Kalnzeem.

(Diary)   *Poor fishing.*

The next day was comparatively good weather,
and I got a few perch and, with the luck that pursued
me on this trip, lost yet another pike.

Wednesday August 20th   Babit S.W. Entrance.

(Diary) *Under power to Babit S.W. entrance.*

On arrival lost my little Aerial reel overboard.

No wind but a fine day. The water was clear and looking down from our bows I saw a glint on the bottom. I took our long lumberman's pole and planted it close by the glint, got the Cook to hold it steady, and slid down it to the bottom and so recovered my knife. I told the Cook, "That's twice it's happened. There'll be a third time, and then I shan't be so lucky." I towed Racundra out, started the motor and steamed down the river to the southwest entrance to the Babit. We anchored and tucked away the sails, and then I set about putting my tackle up ready to catch a fish or two for supper. I had put my rod up on deck and was just putting on my favourite reel, a little aluminium Aerial that I had had for ten years when it slipped from my hands, bumped on the deck and was gone into four fathom of water to a bottom of deep black mud. That was the end of that. It was the third time. I had no further fear of losing things overboard, and lost nothing else during the cruise. But I would have preferred to lose either spectacles or knife.

Thursday August 21st   Babit S.W. Entrance.

(Diary) *Got up still asleep & sailed in dinghy up river mistaken for Babit, to get milk. Got good cream.*

Caught lunch.

E. caught a pike on a reel 4 x gut fishing for perch. Pike hooked deep, caught at corner of jaw so he could not bite. He bit me when I unhooked him.

Heavy rain and thunderstorms in the night.

I got up still asleep and sailed away in the dinghy as I thought up the cut and round the bend into the Babit Sea but actually in the opposite direction back into the main river, where I got milk from a farm on the bank, observed with pleasure that we could easily bring Racundra there and did not discover my ridiculous mistake until the Cook asked me on my return why I had not, as I had meant to do, explored the cut to see if we could take Racundra further up it. This, I think, is my prize effort in navigation, and the Cook has not yet allowed me to hear the last of it. We had a good day's fishing and the Cook caught a nice pike on 4x gut while fishing for perch. I call him a nice pike but as a matter of fact he bit me while I was taking the hook out.

Friday August 22nd   Babit S.W. Entrance.

(Diary) *Heavy rain & thunderstorms in night.*
Strong N.W. wind all day.
Remained at anchor working.
Walked across marshes up to knees in water.
Got milk from farm which was part of the front line.
Pike & perch for lunch with fresh ersh soup.

Remained at anchor.

(Handwritten notes)

Friday August 22nd

After a wearing night of high wind and violent thunderstorms, lightning and thunderclaps close on each others heels and lighting the cabin as at midday, we found a wind that was no good for us going to Scholk, where we had decided to take Racundra to provision her for an expedition to the Babit Sea.

We lay at anchor and I worked all morning.
Our nightlines were a complete failure. After an admirable midday dinner of pike and perch, I went up the mizzenmast to look out over the reeds and the surrounding country. About a mile and a half away over the marshland were several buildings, and the Cook put me ashore with the milk can and the camera.

I found that what had looked like dry land was grass, ankle deep in water. The many haystacks were built on legs to keep them above the level of the marshes and the only road was the edge of a ditch with barbed wire entanglements in it left from the war. I waded along the edge of this ditch, which was dryer than the surrounding fields, and after half an hour's walking came to the beginnings of a road made of branches laid in the mud. The water had only once come over the tops of my knee-boots. By the beginnings of my road were ruins of the old wiring entanglements, a potato patch, a scrap of cornfield, a ruined farm and a new wooden house being built, it was already up to the top of the windows. Hollyhocks were growing along what had obviously been a wartime trench; little untidy buildings, partly refurbished ruins, lived in pending the finishing of the new houses, had a background of low dunes with the broken trunks of trees, lopped and pruned to gaunt sticks by shellfire. In one of the barns I found an old man who quieted the usual raging dogs and told me, also as usual, that he had no milk. But he took me to his wife and daughter who were knitting in a small hut with six beds round its walls, and they told me that though all their milk had already gone through the machine (the separator), their neighbours probably had some. I clambered over some of the ruins to the next building, and then found a barn door with two old men leaning against the two doorposts. I told them what I wanted. They called for a girl to bring some milk, and then began to talk of other things. "Yes the old front line passed through this very place and there had been much fighting in the marshes". When they came back after the war they had found nothing but a flat place where their farm had been, and the ruined foundations of the outbuildings. They were living in them. "Did I think there would be another war?" No. They also thought that such a thing could never occur again. "Everybody was to loose by it. No. In our lifetimes, while people remember, it can never happen again. No one would allow it."

The girl brought the can really full of milk, more than the two measures for which I asked and for which alone they charged. I paid ten roubles a measure. In Riga it is sixteen, and along the river in different places the price varies between 15 and 9.

I waded back over the marshland. The storks had already sought their chimneys or other observation posts for the night. The country stretched flat and green with shining patches of water, and tall reeds, and little round haystacks. Far away I could see Racundra's two masts among the reeds, and, keeping my eyes on these, I waded home to the edge of the ditch, and was ferried home in the dinghy, which answered my hail.

The Cook says there is no point in living in Racundra, that only children are glad to live in a ship, that there is nothing to see, nothing to write about, and that she's sick of wind and rain and living in a small cabin; that I grow worse with age, and that proper authors live at home and write books out of their heads.

A ditch with barbed wire entanglements.

Heavy rain and thunderstorm in the night. Remained at anchor working. It occurs to me that this is the first entry of this kind in the log. As a matter of fact I have been working more or less all the time only it has not occurred to me to chronicle the speed of my typewriter in knots, nor to set down the distance covered in ink over white paper. The nightline we had set last night was a complete failure besides tangling itself in the anchor chain when we swung.

After an admirable midday dinner of yesterday's pike and perch, I went up the mizzenmast to look out over the reeds and the surrounding country. About a mile and a half away over the flat land were several buildings. I reported this and was settling down to my pipe when I observed that the Cook, making no remarks, was putting the milk can in the dinghy. A minute or two later I was put ashore.

It was lucky that I was wearing sea boots, for I found that what had looked like dry land was grass, ankle deep in water. The very haystacks dotted about were built on legs to keep them above the level of the marsh and the only road was the edge of a ditch with barbed wire entanglements left by the war. I waded along the edge of this ditch, which was dryer than the surrounding fields, and after half an hour's serious walking, during which the water only once came over the tops of my knee-boots, I came to the beginning of a road made of branches laid loose in the mud. This road, along which I splashed rather more hopefully, led through the ruins of

The girl brought the milk.

old barbed wire, a potato patch in which the potato plants were
reflected in the gutters between the rows, a scrap of actual
cornfield, and a ruined farm, beside which a new log house was
being built and had already risen to the level of the old windows.
Hollyhocks were in flower along what had obviously been a
wartime trench. Little untidy buildings, old ruins, roughly made
habitable during the building of the new house had a background
of low dunes with broken trunks of trees, lopped and pruned to
gaunt sticks by shellfire. In a broken down barn I found an old
man who, when he had quieted the usual raging dogs, told me the
usual thing, that he had no milk. But he took me to his wife and
daughter who were knitting in what had been a small dug out with
six beds round its walls, and they told me that though all their
milk had already gone through the machine (the separator) their
neighbours probably had some. I clambered over some of the ruins
to the next building, and there found a barn door with part of a
barn behind it. Two old men were leaning against the doorposts,
one each side. I told them what I wanted. They called with
authority to a fine looking girl to bring some milk, and then began
to talk of other things. "Yes the old front line had lain through
their farm. They had had to leave and there had been much
fighting in the marshes. When they came back after the war they
had found nothing but ruins, a flat place where their farm had
been, and the foundations of some of the outhouses. They had
patched these up and were living in them. Did I think there would
be another war? They were afraid, but they thought not. Such a
thing as that could not happen twice. Everybody had lost by it. No.

I was ferried home in the dinghy.

In our lifetimes, while people remembered, it could not happen again. No one would allow it."

The girl brought the milk and they gave me more than the two measures, for which alone they charged. I paid ten roubles a measure. In Riga the price is sixteen, and in different places along the river the price varies from nine to fifteen.

I waded back over the marshland. The storks had left the haystacks and their frog hunting and had gone to seek their chimneys and other observation posts for the night. The country stretched flat and green with shining patches of water, and tall reeds, and little round haystacks on four legs. Far away I could see Racundra's two masts among the reeds, and, keeping my eyes on these, I waded home to the edge of the cut, and was ferried home in the dinghy when the Cook heard my hail.

Saturday August 23rd   Scholk.

(Diary)   *Got up at 4.30. Sailed 4.50 to Shlok.*
          Good S.W. wind promised.
          Glass rising fast. Thunder clouds from N. in afternoon,
          coming up against the S.W. wind which blew up hard
          in minutes.

Back to Scholk.

Remembering the shallow bend and twisting channel between
Pawassern and Frankendorf, and having it firmly in my head that
there was a strong north wind coming, I had made up my mind
to be up early and snatch the hour of peace that there usually is
about dawn to bring Racundra down river to Scholk under the
motor, as the Cook refuses absolutely to go to the Babit Sea without
a visit to town for provisions, her faith in my fishing having fallen
even more than the barometer. At four fifteen in the morning
I woke, put my head on deck into a thick white mist, paler than the
light, for the sun was not yet up and found smooth water and a
mild westerly wind. Ten minutes later I was dressed and on deck.
The Cook slept below, and I moved as quietly as I could, taking the
cover off the mainsail and getting it up. I got the staysail hanked
on the stay and fastened to the sheets and staysail halyard ready
to hoist but tied in a bundle out of the way on the top of the great
anchor. I lashed the tiller to get away on the port tack and took in
chain till the anchor was straight up and down. Then I hauled up
and broke out the staysail, chose my moment, swung the anchor
off the ground and got it aboard, and hurried back to the tiller. She
took an unconscionable time to gather way and we slid nearer and
nearer to the reeds. However, just when I thought that difficulties
were unavoidable she began to draw ahead and away from the
reeds, and a moment later with a good puff of wind was sailing
cleanly out of the cut. There was hardly anything to be seen but
mist. Standing on the afterdeck with my foot on the tiller I could
see over the rising mist to low, purple, fire-rimmed clouds in the
east over the marshes and when we had been sailing ten minutes
and were out into the river the sun came up like the half of a red-
hot penny stuck in this purple bar. The mist curled up from the
surface of the water and rolled northwards in the way we wanted
to go, but at first there was scarcely wind to keep the mainsheet
taut and the boom out. We moved at the pace of a barge drawn by
a very sleepy horse, and, smoking the first pipe of the day, leaning
over the mizzen boom and watching the steaming marshland on
either side of us I felt the perfect bargee and enjoyed myself.
This was not like those other moments sailing Racundra by night
with sleeping crew over a wide sea, with fifty miles before us on
a single tack, but something quite different, quiet, intimate, and
delightful in its different way.

Only the early things were stirring. At the riverside farm milk-
maids were bringing home the cows. A hawk, a marsh harrier
I think, like the one I saw at Wolgund was skimming low over the
reeds. Here and there along the edge of the reeds I saw little fish,
leaping, splash, splash, splash, in their frenzy to escape from a
breakfasting pike. Swifts were getting something from the actual

A boat with four men was laying out a net.

reeds, clinging to the slim rushes like little creepers or nuthatchers,
gathering, I fancy, late sleeping dragonflies. A company of hooded
crows were searching the marsh as if by concerted plan, each for
himself, but between them covering the whole ground. Their flight
when at this sort of serious business is curiously like hawks,
a stroke or two of the wings and then a curving glide. In the dim
white mist up the river a boat with four men was laying out a net.
I heard but could not see the splash of the great anchor. Then,
as Racundra slipped towards them, I saw the boat rowing a wide
circle, paying out the net with its line of corks on the water, and so
back to the starting point, when the rowers rested and the men in
bow and stern began at once winding in the net on a pair of two
handed wooden capstans. As I passed them I saw the little silver
fish gleaming in the net, bleak, for the most part, which they
smoke and send to Riga in full boxes by the steamers. On a half
ruined wooden pier an early, intent little boy, rubbing his bare feet
together from the cold, was fishing with a long peeled, white rod.

On this reach I was almost closehauled, so, lashing the tiller and
letting Racundra sail herself, I took the cover off the mizzen and
hoisted the sail. The mist rose swiftly now, and we were moving
faster through the water and presently would be at that
treacherous bend where we had stirred the mud with our
centreboard on the way up river. I noticed a pair of posts on the
mainland on the left bank and beyond them another pair, that
did not look like telegraph posts and might, perhaps, be leading
marks for the steamers, of course not marked on our map. Yes.
The first pair was visibly closing, and with the glasses I could see
lanterns fixed to their tops. I got them in line, swung the booms
wide and turned sharply to starboard, slipping closely past the little
islands of weeds in the open bend of the river. Then the other two

*The ferry with market carts on board it
was crossing the river.*

came in line, and I jibed, turning to starboard again, and presently
the factory above Scholk was open of the last of the weed islands
and jibing again Racundra was heading clear down the middle of
the river for the little town with its crazy wooden watchtower for
the fire brigade.

A tug I knew with a tow of empty barges passed us going up river
to Mitau. Her skipper got his glasses out and I got mine, and after
having a good look at each other, we exchanged a wave of the
hand. The ferry with market carts on board it was crossing the
river at Scholk, the men leaning on the wooden grips with which
they clutch and pull on the wire rope that runs from side to side
across the bottom of the river. Close below the ferry I jibed again
and rounded to forty yards from the reeds, hauling the mizzen
amidships and bringing the main boom aboard, letting go staysail
sheets, running forward, getting down and stowing the staysail,
and then as we stopped and began to sheer sideways dropping the
anchor in two fathom of water and paying out chain as quietly as
I could. Then a pull on all the topping lifts, and I dropped my
peaks, leaving the sails up to dry the morning dew out of them,
and went below. The Cook was waking. "Are we sailing?" she asked,
"or are you just getting in the anchor chain?" I told her to look out
of the cabin window and be convinced we were at Scholk. As usual
her mind leapt sharply to the practical. "They are turning out the
cows at that farm on the bank. They have just milked. If you get
some milk I'll have breakfast ready by the time you are back."
So I put mast and sail in the little dinghy, and, in the sunshine
that was rapidly drying the dew off the thwarts, I sailed away
for the morning milk, looking back from time to time at Racundra,
that proper little ship, lying demurely in her new anchorage.

Sunday & Monday August 24th & 25th

Scholk.

(Diary, *E. Mitau.*
 Sun)
         Worked.

(Diary, *Worked.*
 Mon)
         E. Mitau.

Tuesday to Friday August 26th to 29th

Babit S.W. Entrance.

(Diary, *Went 3 times to Scholk.*
 Tues)
         Sailed to Babit.

(Diary, *Explored Babit a little early evening.*
 Weds)
         Caught 1 pike in evening about 3-4 lbs.

(Diary, *E. caught pike.*
 Thurs) *Good lot of fish. Soup & fish.*

         Met the marshman in a canoe coming thro' reed alley.

         Saw otter? or v. large water rat.

         Double hump in water when swimming.

(Diary, *Returning from milk getting, saw a female sparrow hawk*
 Fri)   *take a frog a few yards away. Saw a*
         good lot of perch. Fished just at dusk, well.

         Saw otter? Running in waterlily reeds, lifting up his
         stoat-like head, showing white throat. Reed living
         birds much worried by him. Little coot in a hurry walked
         along in front of him, with much squawking in the reeds.

A huge haystack on two boats.

Saturday August 30th   Scholk & ferry.

  (Diary)   *Went to town.*

  (Log)   *Got away 9.30. Rowed out.*

Fish traps to catch fish leaving the Babit.

Sunday to Wednesday August 31st to September 3rd

Babit S.W. Entrance.

(Diary)   *Fine sail to the Babit against the wind.*

*Reaching round the shallow bend below Scholk,
met a huge haystack on two boats, sailing with the
wind, a man on top steering with long pole which
he had moved to the middle of the boat.*

Fished lot of perch.

(Diary,   *5 good fish, a large one grabbed E's float of*
Mon)   *white celluloid & ran out line & hung on for
some time after she began reeling him in.*

*No perch caught after 5 today. The catch was
between 12 & 3.*

(Log)   *Sept.1. Babit. Whilst we were fishing a canoe of
wagoners came to the island opposite us. They all four
paddled kneeling in the canoe, so that as it passed we
wondered what they had done with their legs, as it
looked as if they were standing in a canoe only a few
inches deep.*

*Fish trap to catch the fish leaving the shallow Babit for
the river is set from one side to the other of the shallow
entrance. The same thing in the narrow cut to my milk
woman. This morning I had to go to the opposite side of
Babit and had to paddle through weeds and waterlilies
to get milk.*

Tremendous evening rise.

(Log)   *Wed. Sailed to entrance of Babit.*

Thursday September 4th   Exit of Cook. New Dubbeln.

(Diary) *MOUSE. Flight of Cook. Sailed & motored to*
        Dubbeln. Thence by train.

(Log)   *Thursday. 12. Steamed away because of mouse.*

        Scholk – Waltershof.
        N shore reedy meadows. Forest behind.
        S shore high with pine wooded area.
        3.25. E Babit entrance.

        Anita. Paddle steamer
        Adler. -Ditto-
        Condor. Screw steamer with big open tin chimney
        forward, dangling a dinghy over her counter.

At anchor by New Dubbeln.

The cruise has ended or is on the point of death. I am alone in
Racundra, or rather not quite alone. I am alone with a mouse,
which has sent the whole six foot three of the Cook, undaunted
hitherto by anything but calms, in headlong flight to Riga. The
discovery was made this morning. I woke at five and heard what
I thought was unmistakeable mouse, but, believing it rather good
luck, besides being a miracle, I said nothing about it, did not wake
the Cook and went fishing. When I came back I mentioned it and
got into rather a row for even pretending such a thing. I went
fishing again and in about an hour heard the foghorn going from
Racundra, so hurried back. The Cook keeps things for darning
under her mattress. A pair of half darned stockings of mine had
been found there, gnawed all to pieces, a mass of heather mixture
fluff, most perfect for any mouse particular about its bedding. The
Cook was convinced and was for starting for Riga at once. This
determination was presently petrified and steel bound when she
found a crowd of its footprints, little three-toed paddy marks in
the stiff sour cream. We started just as we were, the dinghy full
of fishing rods and tackle. I started the engine, and so came out of
the entrance to the Babit and round the shallow bend above Scholk
where the wind was against us, and thereafter sailed, tidying up
as we went along. There was little wind and, as the Cook absolutely
refused to sleep on board again, I started the engine again and
badly burnt two of my fingers, which makes writing difficult.

At half past six we were just coming near Dubbeln where for a hundred yards or so the railway skirts the river. I shouted to a man to know when the next train went for Riga. We had twenty minutes. The Cook was dressed for Riga in ten. In fifteen we were close to the station, which is on the very bank of the river. I rounded up, dropped the anchor to hold temporarily, rowed like the boatrace for the embankment. The Cook hared up it and crossed the line just in front of the engine and was gone and I paddled back to Racundra, got my anchor again, chose a decentish berth, anchored again for the night, stowed the sails, ate two three-quarter pound perch of my own catching and a large bar of chocolate, opened a bottle of beer, which stands beside me, and settled down, still a little breathless, to recount these alarums and excursions.

Tomorrow at dawn, the wind being southwest and favourable, as I am pretty well convinced it will be, I shall hoist our sails and proceed. The whole thing is a puzzle. How on earth the mouse got on board is a question my answers to which only increased the desperation of the Cook. We have never touched shore with Racundra since we left Riga, never tied up to a pier. Perhaps a hawk dropped it, flying over us and startled by our flag. Perhaps, swimming across the river, pursued by a pike, it scrambled to safety up the anchor chain. What is the good of looking for ordinary explanations of extraordinary things? Mice do not hatch out from eggs, or it might have been smuggled on board in some minute and inconspicuous form. Why have we never noticed it before? We surely should have done if it had been a passenger with us from the start, as the Cook was inclined to suggest until I pointed out that if so we had got along very well with it so far and why not continue in peace and amity. Two boys of the marshes startled the Cook yesterday by coming alongside in a dugout canoe. Perhaps they threw it into the open forehatch. But what should they be doing with a mouse, and why should they give it to us? I am inclined myself to think that it was brought us as a present by the stork who flew over us every evening on his way home, in a sort of delicate allusion to the stories about himself, as if to make a tiny joke at his own expense.

However that may be, the cruise is all but over. The Cook has gone, and I am left a hero to face the raging lion in a mouse's skin.

Friday September 5th   New Dubbeln – Bilderlingshof.

(Diary)   *Sailed Dubbeln to Bilderlingshof.*
          Went through the bridge.

          Evening Cook returned, ashamed, with mousetraps.

(Log)   *Sept 5. Thick fog in morning. Sailed in a calm 10.30*
          as soon as banks visible.
          No mousetraps at Dubbeln even at Jews.

There was a thick fog in the morning. I went ashore and from
one end to the other of the little town of Dubbeln, trying to buy
a mousetrap. The people of Dubbeln are indifferent to mice or
perhaps the Hamlin piper visited that place and took the mice
away with him. The people of Dubbeln were surprised at my
enquiry and sent me from one shop to another and I went
obediently whither I was directed up and down that long street of
little shops. I asked for mousetraps at the shops with gaudy pillars
twined about with stripes of many colours, where they sell paints.
I tried at the shops where they hang out a picture of a grey bath
and a yellow tap. I tried at the shops where the signs show top
boots. Finally, in desperation, I went to the shop which hangs out
a golden double twisted roll. Surely, I thought, the baker must be
afflicted by mice, and if he does not sell traps, at least he will know
where to buy them. But the baker's wife put her handkerchief
straight on her head, and gave herself up to thought. After a
minute she said. "You will not find a mousetrap in Dubbeln, unless
it is in the little iron shop belonging to the Jew." She told me where
to find the Jew. He was not in the main street but in one of the
little sandy alleyways, and I could not find him. So maybe there
is a mousetrap in Dubbeln after all. I felt rather nervous about
leaving Racundra alone in the fog, and so, despairing of finding
the Jew, which finding seemed to be the only hope of finding
a mousetrap, I hurried back to my dinghy and paddled away in the
mist, stern first, looking for Racundra who was, I knew, somewhere
in the direction of the sun. I caught at last the dim line of a mast
and of a smaller one beside it, and presently the whole ghost of
my little ship was close to me in the fog. The decks were wet and
slippery and the dew stood in beads on the covers of the sails.
There was nothing to be seen from her but white fog. I smoked
a pipe and came again on deck, and could see in the fog a little
patch of reeds with their reflections in the milky water. There was

no wind. At half past ten I could just see the banks, and the sun
was already much less like a lamp in cotton wool. So I took the
covers off the sails and hoisted them. There was the faint breath
of wind from the northwest and I got the anchor, and making
one board on the starboard tack, went about and with the wind
free headed down stream. The fog turned to mist and was gone,
suddenly. The sun shone out and the wind from the northwest took
heart though not much, and down the eastern arm of the Dubbeln
bend, Racundra sailed goose-winged, her mizzen boom to starboard,
her main boom to port, the wind dead aft, and her master and
owner wishing he could project himself a hundred yards ahead
to see her so, bearing down upon him as he had watched with
admiration the Esthonian schooners flying goose winged from the
Moon Sound. At this moment we met the Toka, a cutter from the
Riga club, sailing to Mitau. There was a man at the tiller, another
tending the mainsheet, others taking care of jib and staysail sheets,
and a number of bright knitted jumpers and white shoes on board,
and they came towards us with a cheerful clatter of tongues. And
we, goose winged, bore down upon them in silent pride, Racundra,
her master and owner, and the mouse, who was busy somewhere
below. We passed a few yards distant from each other and
exchanged greetings. They were bound for Mitau with a crew of
thirteen. Round the Dubbeln bend the wind came again on our
port side, and with staysail mizzen and main all drawing well, in
the easy wind, we slipped down the long reach to Bilderlingshof
and the railway bridge that had kept us waltzing for so long
waiting for someone to speak the "Open Sesame". This time
I was determined not to wait inactive but to find out the seemingly
incomprehensible laws of the bridge's hours for opening and
shutting. So I sailed close to the bridge and rounded up on the
windward side of the river thirty yards from a boat landing,
dropped the anchor and leaving all sails standing except the
staysail, tumbled into the dinghy and went ashore. I ran up the
embankment to the bridge-keeper's hut and asked when the
bridge would be open.

"There won't be a steamer till four or five o'clock in the afternoon."

"Are there fixed times for the opening and shutting of the bridge,
for if so I would like to have them, so as to know for the future."

"No. There are no fixed times. We open whenever there is
a necessity."

I looked at Racundra lying there waiting to go through. As if she
were not deserving of an opened bridge as much as any penny
steamer. But rhetoric would have been wasted on the bridge-keeper.
I pulled a Lat from my pocket, the equivalent of an English shilling

and showed it to the bridge-keeper.

"Is this what you would call a necessity?" I asked. He took it.

"A train is just due," he said, "But as soon as it is passed we will open the bridge. It will be open by the time you are ready for it."

So I hurried back to Racundra, ran up the staysail, got the anchor on board again just as the train passed, and a moment later the bridge swung open and Racundra slid through. I went across to the southern side of the river, sounded and found five fathom, then, feeling my way along the channel, presently settled on a good anchorage, in two fathoms, near enough to the reed beds to be out of the way of the timber rafts and tugs. Going under the bridge, the tugs take off their hats as they go through, and are not, like the steamers, compelled to keep to the left side of the river, where the bridge opens. I stowed the sails, put the covers on, and poached some eggs.

Saturday September 6th Bullen – Bilderlingshof.

> (Diary) *Leslie came. Sailed to Bolderaa.*
>
> *Evening sail in dinghy.*

Sunday September 7th   Bilderlingshof – Babit S.W.

> (Diary) *Mouse caught*
>
> *Cook therefore agreed to go to Mitau & back.*
>
> *Sailed from Bilderlingshof at 12 noon. Calm.*
> *Donkey all the way, to Babit S.W. under power.*
>
> (Log) *Sept 7. Sunday. Calm. Through bridge 12 noon.*
> *Babit S.W. entrance 7.45.*
> *Stopped Schaggern to see Babit Lake*
> *& by Kesa a meeting Toka*
> *& at Waltershof to replenish kerosene.*

Monday September 8th

Babit S.W. – Mitau.
(Diary) Babit S.W. – Mitau
Under sail.
Motor in last reach before Mitau
on account of dead calm.

(Log)   *Sept 8.   Monday*

Sailed 7.10. Wind strong S.W.
Out of Babit Lake 7.30.
Below Kalnzeem went through shallows marked
by 2 spar buoys.

Kalnzeem ferry.	*10.15 Wind strengthening from S.W.*
Umul.	*11. Wind backing to N.W.*
Wreck at Ratneek.	*12.15. Wind shifting.*
Wolgund.	*12.45. Wind dropping.*
Steamer Jurmalmiks.	*2. By Bruwer.*
Bruwer.	*2.30.*
Plerren.	*2.45. Motored up to left hand bank where remains of ferry and bridge are.*
	Rain storm & shifting wind.

Beyond Plerren and Plane we saw 2 men a woman
and a cat catching perch with a fishing net. The cat got
her fish and returned with it unharmed thinking her
prize might or not be held a privilege.

Ekau River.	*4. No wind.*
Started motor when it had started raining.	
Mitau.	*5.30.*

Tuesday September 9th

Mitau – Bilderlingshof.

(Diary) *Sailed from Mitau 7.55.*

Good wind.

Bilderlingshof at dark.

(Log) *Sept. 9. Mitau.*
Moon in the mist. House by the bridge. Few lights.

Started.	*7.45. Wind S. to S.E.*
Ekau River.	*8.49*
Plerren.	*9.21. Lady ferrying geese.*
Brewen.	*9.34.*
Wolgund	*10.30. Tug with raft coming up river.*
Ratneek. Wind.	*10.37.*
Umul.	*11.22.*
Kalnzeem.	*11.47.*
12 Noon.	*Cook took charge.*
12.45.	*Kumle*
Entrance to Babit.	*1.12.*
Scholk ferry.	*2.06. Hard reach at Scholk bend.*
Babit E. entrance.	*3.10.*
Waltershof.	*3.25.*
Dubbeln.	*4.57.*

Calm between Dubbeln and to Bilderlingshof.
6.30. Slight wind from S.W.
8.10. Through Bilderlingshof Bridge.
Anchored 8.30.
Glass falling about two tenths.

12 Midnight.	*Wind very strong. S.W. Glass falling another 2 tenths. Dinghy wandering about on its warps. Needed tending all the time.*

Wednesday September 10th

Bilderlingshof to Bolderaa
& Dvina to Stint Sea.

(Diary) *Bilderlingshof – Stint See.*

V. strong. S.W. wind.

(Log) *Sept. 10.   Barometer 28.1. Wind strong S.W.*
Left Bilderlingshof.   8.30.
Met paddle tug at Bolderaa.   9.10.
Aground.   9.30.
Sailing.   9.50.

Hard job tacking up Dvina because of nets.

Very hard squalls in Stint Sea.

Anchor down.   1 pm

Prelude to Racundra's Third Cruise

The Dream

Arthur Ransome's 'Racundra's First Cruise' begins with the words:

'Houses are but badly built boats so firmly aground that you cannot think of moving them. They are definitely inferior things, belonging to the vegetable not the animal world, rooted and stationary, incapable of gay transition. I admit, doubtfully, as exceptions, snail-shells and caravans. The desire to build a house is the tired wish of a man content thenceforward with a single anchorage. The desire to build a boat is the desire of youth, unwilling yet to accept the idea of a final resting-place.'

From the time that Arthur Ransome and his lover Evgenia Shelepina started their sailing careers in Estonia early in 1920, he had dreamed of creating the ideal cruising boat and adopting a more normal lifestyle than that of itinerant war correspondent and journalist. By the time Racundra's Third Cruise came to be written he had realised this dream in its fullest extent. Racundra had been built and he had entered into a lifelong permanent relationship with Evgenia.

His diary for 1921 records:

(Diary) 15 April

In the evening went and fell in love with Mr. Eggers,
with the probable result that we shall have a boat built
by him. The enthusiasm of the fellow when he is talking

of a possible boat simply carries me off my feet and hundreds of pounds out of my depth. He proposes a perfect boat to go anywhere single-handed with every kind of tweak. Talked it over with Evgenia who herself is bowled over by Eggers. She too votes for getting his boat.

(Diary) 21 April

Evgenia says she can live until April 21, 1923 with no new clothes?!!!!

Almost exactly a year later in 1922 he wrote in a letter to his mother:

(April 27th) The boat in which I shall cruise will not be ready for sea for another month, which is most annoying, as we shall lose about three weeks of good weather ... it is maddening about her not being ready, when we have been howling at the man, and tinkering and hammering has been going on all winter. However, when she is ready, she will be a really stout ship, and it will be our own fault if accidents occur. I have taken the compass down to be fitted in a good place aft of the mizzen mast and in front of the steering well. Her appearance when ready will be something like this:

The boat is fully described in the Appendix to Racundra's First Cruise:

'Racundra is nine metres over all – something under thirty feet long. She is three and a half metres in beam – nearly twelve feet. She draws three feet six inches without her centreboard, and seven feet six inches when the centreboard is lowered. Her enormous beam is balanced by her shallowness, and though for a yacht it seems excessive, thoroughly justified itself in her comfort and stiffness. She has a staysail, mainsail and mizzen, and for special occasions a storm staysail, a balloon staysail, a small squaresail (much too small), a trysail and a mizzen staysail. She could easily carry a very much greater area of canvas, but, for convenience in single-handed sailing, she has no bowsprit, and the end of the mizzen boom can be reached from the deck.

She is very heavily built and carries no inside ballast. Her centreboard is of oak. She has a three-and-a-half ton iron keel, so broad that she will rest comfortably upon it when taking the mud, and deep enough to enable us to do without the centreboard altogether except when squeezing her up against the wind. Give her a point or two free and a good wind and her drift, though more than that of a deep-keel yacht, is much less than that of the coasting schooners common in the Baltic. With the centreboard down she is extremely handy, and proved herself so by coming successfully through the narrow Nukke Channel with the wind in her face, a feat which the local vessels do not attempt.

But the chief glory of Racundra is her cabin. The local yachtsmen, accustomed to the slim figures of racing boats, jeered at Racundra's beam and weight, but one and all, when they came aboard her, ducked through the companionway and stood up again inside that spacious cabin, agreed that there was something to be said for such a boat. And as for their wives, they said frankly that such a cabin made a boat worth having, and their own boats, which had seemed comfortable enough hitherto, turned into mere uncomfortable rabbit-hutches. Racundra's cabin is a place where a man can live and work as comfortably and twice as pleasantly as in any room ashore. I lived in it for two months on end, and, if this were a temperate climate, and the harbour were not a solid block of ice in winter, so that all yachts are hauled out and kept in a shed for half the year, I should be living in it still. Not only can one stand up in Racundra's cabin, but one can walk about there, and that without interfering with anyone who may be sitting at the writing-table, which is a yard square. In the middle of the cabin is a folding-table four feet by three, supported by the centreboard-case; and so broad is the floor that you can sit at that table and never find the case in the way of your toes. The bunks are wider than is usual, yet behind and above each bunk are two deep cupboards, with between them a deep open space divided by a shelf, used on the port side for books and on the starboard side for crockery. Under the bunks is storage for bottles. Under the flooring on the wide flat keel is storage for condensed milk and tinned food. Behind the bunks, between them and the planking, below the cupboards and book-shelves, is further storage room.

Racundra was designed as a boat in which it should be possible to work, and as a floating study or office, I think it would be difficult to improve upon her. The writing-table is forward of the port bunk, and a Lettish workman made me an admirable little three-legged stool, which, when the ship is under way, stows under the table. Above and behind the ample field of the table is a deep cupboard and a bookcase, of a height to take the Nautical Almanac, the Admiralty Pilots, Dixon Kemp and Norie's inevitable Epitome and Tables. Another long shelf is to be put up along the bulkhead that divides the cabin from the forecastle. Under the shelf for nautical books is a shallow drawer where I keep a set of pocket tools, nails, screws and such things. Under the writing-table is a big chart drawer, where I keep the charts immediately in use, writing and drawing materials, parallel rulers, protractors, surveying compass (Ed. Note: now more usually called a hand-bearing compass), stopwatch and other small gear. By the side of this is a long narrow drawer, used for odds and ends, and underneath that is a special cupboard made to take my portable typewriter. On the starboard side, opposite the table, is space for a stove, which, however, on this cruise we used for stowing spare mattresses (Ed. Note: Ransome was here referring to the first cruise of Racundra; the stove was, however, added for the third cruise.) Behind it are deep cupboards with low coamings to prevent things slipping (Ed. Note: now more usually called fiddles). Here were empty portmanteau, seaboots, and a watertight box for photographic material. The door into the forecastle is on this side, so that it is possible to go through even when someone is sitting at the writing-table. In the forecastle is one full-length comfortable bunk on the port side. On the starboard side there are big cupboards instead of a second bunk. These were used for ship's stores, such as blocks and carpenter's tools, shackles and the rest. A seat is fixed close by the mainmast, to a big central cupboard which is the full height of the forecastle from deck to floor, and was used for oilskins and clothes. In the forecastle we stowed warps, spare anchor, tins of kerosene, one of the water-barrels and the sails. This left small room for the Ancient Mariner, but, as he said, 'There was room to lie and sleep, and room to sit and smoke, and what does any man want with more?' The main cabin is the general living-room.

As you come out of the cabin into the companionway, you find on either hand a cupboard from deck to floor. On the starboard side is a simple and efficient closet, and aft of that, under the deck, a big space used for all the engineering tools, lubricating oils and greases. On the port side is the galley, with room for three primus stoves (I am fitting a Clyde cooker). One of the stoves is in heavy iron gimbals for use when under way. Behind this is a shelf and rack for cooking-things, and aft, under the deck, a second water-barrel. The engine, a heavy oil, hot-bulb Swedish engine, burning kerosene (we have no benzine in the ship), is under the self-draining steering-well. It is completely covered when not in use by a wooden case, contrived to provide steps up to the deck The case takes to pieces, but can be fixed with absolute rigidity, so that people who have visited Racundra have asked on going away, what was the purpose of the reversing lever (at the side of the companionway, within reach of the steering well), never having suspected that we had an engine on board. For all the good we got of it during this first cruise we might just as well have had no engine, but next year I hope to take the engine seriously and learn the Open Sesame that will set it miraculously to work. The oil reservoir is in the extreme stern, and is filled from the deck. The companionway can be completely covered in by a folding and sliding lid, over which we shall have a canvas cover. The raised trunking of the cabin is carried completely round companion, mizzen mast and steering well, so that there is plenty of room inside this coaming for a man to lie full length. In summer this would be a most desirable place to sleep, and even on this autumn cruise, during our days of fine weather, we put one of the spare mattresses there, and anyone who was not busy with some thing else reclined there, smoked, dozed, read or bothered the steersman with irrelevant conversation. The steering-well itself gives room for two people. In front of it, immediately aft of the mizzen mast, is the binnacle, and under the deck, between companion way and steering-well, is a cupboard for riding light, binoculars, fog-horn, etc. The main sheet, mizzen sheet, backstays and staysail sheets are all cleated within easy reach of the steersman, who can do everything but reef without leaving his place. Owing to the height of the narrow mainsail, inevitable in a ketch, the gaff tends to swing too far forward, so I have a vang, which also serves as a downhaul, fastened to the peak, and cleated, when in use, close by the mizzen mast.'

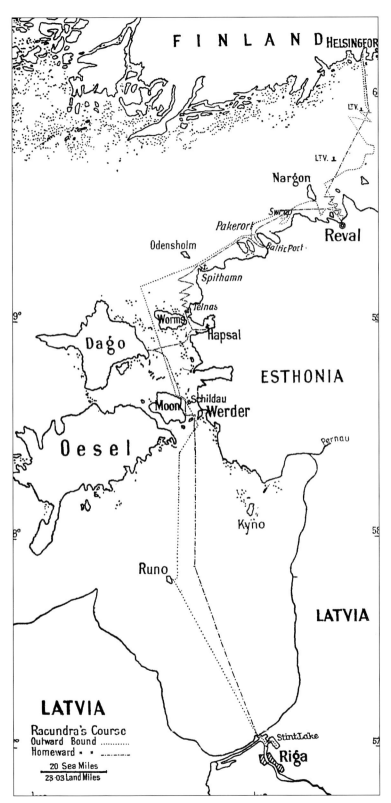

Racunda's First Cruise.

The First Cruise

His dream ship.

'Racundra's First Cruise' took place in August and September 1922. Ransome started to write an account of the trip at Christmas. It was published in July 1923, and was his first really successful book.

Ransome, who later became famous as author of the 'Swallows and Amazons' series of children's books, had been working in Russia, for the Daily News and Manchester Guardian newspapers, at the time of the revolution in 1917 and had fallen in love with Evgenia Shelepina, Trotsky's secretary. Together they sailed in Estonia during 1920 and 1921 in two old and decrepit boats that they had acquired in Reval (now called Tallin).

In August 1921 they left Estonia and moved to Riga in Latvia. Ransome was now financially secure enough to consider having a boat built to his own requirements. He commissioned the Reval yacht designer Otto Eggers to design his dream ship. She was built in a shed on the Stint Sea, a lake at the entrance of the Dvina River, near Riga. The boat should have been ready in April 1922 but with the usual boat builder's delays was not completed until mid August. Even then Ransome had to complete much of the work himself. It has been said that the only boat builder to complete a boat on time was Noah!

The Crew was Ransome...

...the Cook (Evgenia)...

...and the Ancient Mariner (Carl Sehmel).

They finally set sail on August 20th, sailed to the Island of Runö through the Moon Sound to Reval and on to Helsingfors returning to Riga on September 26th. The crew was Ransome, the Cook (Evgenia) and the Ancient Mariner (Carl Sehmel). Sehmel was the boatman who looked after small boats on the Stint Sea and helped Ransome with fitting out Racundra. The origin of the name Racundra is said to be Ra (Ransome), c (Carl), und (and), ra (Evgenia – who was not yet a Ransome).

The cruise was highly eventful. They had problems with the compass, sails (having broken the gaff jaws), the engine (a love hate relationship with the skipper) and last but not least the weather.

While describing a particularly bad gale Ransome wrote:

'The Cook struggled up the companionway with a sandwich. She asked with real inquiry, "Are we going to be drowned before morning?"
I leaned forward from the steering-well and shouted, "Why?"
"Because I have two thermos flasks full of hot coffee. If we are,
we may as well drink them both. If not, I'll keep one till tomorrow."
We kept one.'

On returning to Riga Racundra was laid up for the winter.

The couple were living in rented accommodation at 23 Stralsunder Strasse, Kaiserwald. During February 1923 Ransome went to Moscow on business and while he was away the house caught fire. On the February 24th he wrote to his mother:

15, Stralsunder Strasse,
Kaiserwald,
Riga.
Feb.24 1923

My dearest Mother,

Please observe number of street. 23 Stralsunder Strasse no
longer exists. Nothing is left but charred logs, and a chimney
with bits of the lower storey.

I have lost almost everything: new evening clothes not yet worn,
all my boots and shoes except the one old pair I took to Moscow,
your lovely clock, my sextant, and every single thing belonging
to the boat, all the sails, all the ropes, all the wire rigging, all
the lamps, every single thing, even the tiller, which for safety
I had taken home. Nothing is left of the boat but the bare hull
in the Yacht Club. About two hundred pounds worth of stuff
gone. I suppose it would cost at least a hundred pounds to get
again all the boat things, and even if I were to order the sails
and ropes at once, I doubt if I could get them in time for the
summer. That means that not only is the boat useless for
a year but that I cannot get a second book to follow the first.

Generally the disaster is pretty complete.

Walking about among the frozen ruins I have picked up two
shackles, and the twisted bottom of my beloved cabin lamp,
and a small bit of iron rigging. That is all.

What was not burnt was stolen by the fire brigade, who even
saved camera cases, from which the cameras had miraculously
disappeared, and were actually seen by a neighbour smashing
open the sextant box with a hatchet and breaking the sextant
in doing so after it had been saved undamaged from the wreck.

I am too gloomy to write more for the moment.

This is the first time that the possibility of another book about
Racundra is mentioned.

The Second Cruise

The writing of the Racundra's First Cruise and other journalistic activities kept Ransome busy until July when he set sail for a trip around the Finnish islands. They cruised from Riga to Helsinki and then spent until September cruising the Finnish islands in the southwest of the country. Carl Sehmel's daughter reports that during the cruise Evgenia would sleep with a grass snake wrapped round her breasts!

Following the success of the first book Ransome had hoped that the proposed cruise to Finland would provide material for a second volume. To achieve this an accurate deck log was kept and, from this, narrative of the cruise was typed up as they went. The cruise, however, did not go according to plan. The day after they arrived in Tallin (Reval), July 25th, Ransome received a telegram summoning him to an urgent meeting in London. He was not able to return and set sail for Helsinki (Helsingfors) until August 21st. They then spent a week there delayed by bad weather and engine problems in spite of having had the engine serviced in Tallin. Rafsö at the southwestern end of the Finnish archipelago was reached on August 28th. They spent a week there riding out a S. W. gale. Ransome recalls this period in handwritten notes included with his typescript:

> *Then followed a southerly gale, which lasted a week, and kept us busy with our anchors, in shelter as we were. We fished whenever possible as we had no other food. I caught quantities of good perch and a small pike on a frog on my finest perch tackle. We saw the summer slipping from us, and watched the summer residents of the islands being given trips to Helsingfors on the local cabs with their furniture, the local cabs being motor fishing boats.*
>
> *Sept. 4. A doubtful day of W. or N.W. wind.*
> *We ought to have started and got at least across to Reval.*

Ransome recorded the cruise in some 6000 words of typescript. Apart from the first part of the trip, his enforced stay in Tallin, and the laying up of Racundra the majority of the writing is mostly a factual account of courses, weather and the day-to-day routine of cruising. At what point he abandoned the idea of turning it into a book is not known. It may well have been on his return to Tallin on September 6th when he discovered that he had to go immediately to Moscow on urgent journalistic business.

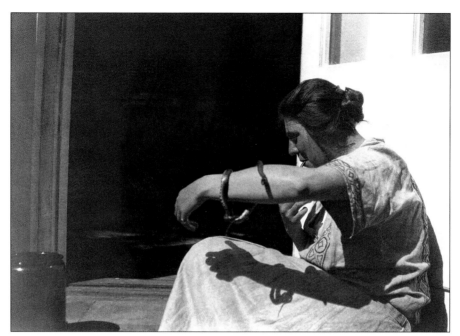

*A fourth member of the crew, a grass snake,
name of Oureberes.*

The first part of the voyage Ransome titled:

Riga to Rohukulla

July 18.

Racundra this year ships a fourth member of the crew, a grass
snake from Moscow over a yard long with a passion for frogs
and the name of Oureberes. He takes his name from 'The Worm
Oureberes', a romance by E.R. Eddison, which will some day
take its rightful place with Mededith's 'Shaving of Shagpat'
and Beckford's 'Vathek'. Oureberes travels in a huge jam-jar,
crawls hither and thither on deck and over the cabin table and
is happiest curled round and round the bottom of the teapot.
The rest of the crew is unchanged except that it is a year older
than it was, by calendar reckoning, but agrees unanimously that
it feels more than a year younger after its pleasant adventures
last year. The crew consists, accordingly, of the Cook, the Ancient
Mariner, Oureberes and the Master.

We left the harbour in the Stint See at 10.30 with a light, fluky
wind, W. and W. by N. shifting presently to the eastwards, and
comparing our trim setting sails, our new cream paint, our
glittering rigging screws, with our condition at our start last year
when we were actually belaying foresheets to mizzen shrouds
because the cleats were not yet bolted to the decks, when our

I took photographs of the ship while the Ancient steered.

topsides were merely smeared with oil and ochre, when our sails hung anyhow, we were quite as proud as was good for us. We wriggled through the Mühlgraben canal without touching, found old friends at the Customs House, made our way out into the river, where I dropped into the dinghy and took photographs of the ship while the Ancient steered. At half past three we delivered up our ticket of leave to the man on the little quay at Dunamunde, carrying it to him in the dinghy as the cables of a dredger prevented us from approaching the pier, and by four o'clock were clear of the moles and at sea. The wind was N.N.E. and very slight, but, rejecting the idea of anchoring in the river we crawled slowly out, until at 6.30 we passed the first howling buoy having made good something over a mile an hour.

A three masted schooner dressed with flags was towed out after us by a little steamer, similarly gay and cast off the towropes about a mile away from us. She was probably bound on a long voyage for people on the steamer were playing Lettish airs on trumpets, someone on the schooner was trying to keep time with them on an accordion, the crew were singing, and when at last the steamer turned back, off on its course to the north east, probably going to Hainasch, there was a general fusillade of pistol shots.

At ten o'clock the Riga great lighthouse bore 145 deg. on my prismatic compass. The calm was absolute. The water glassy.

6. calm.

6.30. wind fair all night, slight puffs.

Sighted Runo. N.N.W. not long from...

Sea licht a shallow patch. 1½ mile S.E of Runö.

Saw water spout.

... N.W. swell. wind N.N.W.

*Suddenly we noticed what looked like
a straight India rubber tube.*

Two hours later the schooner was so near us that we used our
long lumberman's pole as a sweep to turn Racundra's head.
Do what we could the ships seemed attracted by each other
like magnets and we had much ado to prevent the schooner's
bowsprit from investigating our rigging. The night was
absolutely still, except for fitful dancing on the deck of the
becalmed schooner and the occasional flap of a sail.

At 1.30 we got a little wind from the south, and made good about
four miles before it died. We were glad enough to be quit of the
schooner, which sailed a course more westerly than ours, evidently
making for Domesness and the open Baltic and meaning to pass
between Runö and the mainland.

Calms in the Baltic are always ominous and though Racundra
is a much better ship than some of the others I have been
caught out in here, we were none of us too pleased to see that
the barometer was falling fast.

At daylight we got a little more wind now from the southwest.
Riga was still in sight, bearing south. At 3.35 streamed log, reading
32. At six thirty we passed the outer spar buoy. Ten miles out
from Riga. At 11.15 the log read 50. We had made 18 miles and a
little more. At six we were again in a dead calm but with a heavy
swell from the northwest. At six thirty we were suddenly moving
fast again, in a series of short squalls which kept us continually

shifting the booms and working with the sheets as in the course of ten minutes we had the wind from all different quarters. Then we sighted Runö Island, fifty miles out from Riga bearing N.N.W.

At the same moment we saw not far away seabirds feeding on a small patch of obviously shallow water, which, as it is marked on the chart gave us an absolute fix of our position. A moment or two later we saw a thing that is very rarely seen in these waters. Indeed the Ancient said he had never seen one outside the Indian Ocean. Away to westwards was a heavy dark strip of cloud, with clear greenish sky beneath it. Suddenly we noticed what looked like a straight India rubber tube connecting the dark cloud with the sea and moving rapidly between cloud and sea, towards us, as it seemed. It was of course very hard to judge its distance, but we thought it must be something over half a mile in height. I closed down the companion hatchway, but the Ancient said there was small use in doing that, "for if one of them water spouts touches a ship it'll break it like a matchbox." And then as we watched the thing it seemed to twist, to be drawn out, to be twirled like a huge corkscrew, and thus waltzing towards us, while still at a great distance, it twisted itself asunder in the middle. Part of it seemed to go upwards to the cloud and the great body of it to fall into the sea, like a subsiding fountain, and (but it may have been our excitement) we all thought we could see the foam mounting up and up from the tremendous splash of its descent. With that we got a good wind and, clearing Runö, set a course to bring us to the mouth of the Sound. At 2.30 a.m. we thought we saw Kano light away to the southeast.

I have never seen a wilder sky at dawn, or one with greater variety of clouds. There were dark clouds like anvils, pillar clouds rising perpendicular from the sea, clouds like jagged swords, clouds of fantastic broken shapes like prehistoric beasts, and clouds like torn out scattered handfuls of white hair. At 6.45 we sighted Kibbosaar and Laiduninna, and bore a little more easterly, bringing the wind nearly dead astern. We met a steamer coming out, and 9 a.m. could see Kuivast in a space between Paternoster and the island of Moon. I took in the log, reading 10 plus 50 plus 18. 78 miles. This is a good deal more accurate than last year especially considering the distance we travelled at a very low speed when the log does not register at all. At ten o'clock we passed Paternoster a hundred miles out from Riga, and were steering for the Shildau buoy.

The wind was strong from the west intensified now and again by angry squalls and we were quickly through the passage marked by the Shildau beacons and steering northwards with the Moon beacons in line astern of us. Now we were in the Sound and were congratulating ourselves on getting here before the weather grew really bad as the sky and the still falling barometer promised. But we were reckoning without the shallow water of the Sound. In the Gulf of Riga with a depth of fifteen, or twenty fathoms, a wind like this could do little to hurt us, but in the Moon with under five fathoms at the deepest part and mostly depths even in the channel of not more than three, this wind lifted a very short breaking sea and when we got the full force of the wind coming between Moon and Dago Racundra, for all her weight, her tremendous beam and her very little sail area was flung over again and again till her cabin roof hit the water, while the seas struck her such blows that it was precisely as if we were colliding with sunken timbers. One of these blows, or the cumulative effect of a number of them split a three-inch square stringer a little forward of the mast. (This I had solidly strengthened at Reval.) To ease her we took off the staysail and the mizzen after which she made easier weather of it. I thought of working westwards to Heltermaa under the weather shore, but the short sea brought her up short and knocked her off her course, so that we could make little headway, and I presently decided to let her fall off and reach for Rukeraga passage, get through that and make for Rohukulla or Hapsal. In any case once through the Rukeraga, we should be in smooth water behind a hidden breakwater of sunken shoals.

We found the Rukeraga beacon without difficulty, shot through the narrow lane of stakes, and steered with the wind dead aft for the leading marks on shore by Rohukulla harbour, the entry into which we could not see till we were close upon it, when, bringing the booms over we rounded into the northern part of the harbour and found plenty of room, and good anchorage in three fathom of water. Made all snug and slept for 14 hours.

The enforced stay in Tallin and trip across the Gulf of Finland to Helsinki is recalled as:

Reval to Helsingfors.

The day after Racundra reached Reval I got a telegram asking me to return immediately to England for a meeting, the date of which scarcely allowed me time to get back. This, of course, knocked on the head my plans for sailing to Petrograd, as I would not risk being held there by the western winds, which one expects here in the autumn. However, there was nothing to be done, so I arranged to have the motor overhauled and the iron horse for the mainsheet put in its place during my absence. I sailed on the Rugen for Stettin, met a yachtsman whose ship had laid alongside my own, had a pleasant voyage, and much enjoyed the entry through Swinemunde and the inland sea. I saw two Yacht Club harbours in the river, and decided to come here sometime in Racundra.

At Stettin I had an hour to spare before the train left for Berlin. I took my bag to the station and then ran back along the quay to a marine stores I had noticed where I found some plain wooden double blocks, not patent, but with easy running brass sheaves, in any case infinitely better than the murderous things with a knife edge division between the sheaves which had been made in Riga. I bought half a dozen of them for the equivalent of six shillings, and caught the train. The ticket from Stettin to Berlin cost less than a shilling. It and the blocks came cheap to me because it just so happened that I had reached Berlin on the morrow of a tremendous fall in the mark. In Berlin I found all tickets for the night train taken, but was rescued by a friend who had a couple, and so reached London via Flushing in time for my appointment. My business in London took two days, and I waited another two in order to come back to Reval with my old friend Captain Whalley on the Baltabor. The Ancient was smoking on deck as we steamed into harbour and we were scarcely tied up to the quay before he was under the stern in the dinghy. We loaded the luggage in and half an hour later were reeving the new blocks.

Still the trip to England had spoilt our cruise, and we were in two minds whether or not to start back for Riga. However, the Cook had never been to Helsingfors, and we remembered last year's oatcakes and decided to run across to Finland, if only for a day.

We had visitors for supper on the evening of August 21, warped out to the buoy and hoisted the main and mizzen while they were still on board, then bundled them unceremoniously ashore and sailed out of the harbour at 9.05 p.m. It was already dark but a fine clear night with a slight westerly wind. Heading directly between Reval high light and the western end of Wulf we were pointing north by our compass. By chart north by west. This however gave us only a slight indication of the compass error caused by the new iron horse immediately before the binnacle. We were to learn afterwards that on other points of sailing the deviation was three times as bad. However with this observation to guide us, we were well enough for the run northwards to Helsingfors. At 11.35 we had the castle lights on Wiems in line, at 2.40 the Surop light was obscured by Nargon, at 3.15 becoming momentarily visible through the trees when, with the Revalstein lighthouse bearing N. by E. $\frac{1}{2}$ E, it gave us an approximate fix of our position. The wind shifted southerly and we brought the booms over. Presently we rigged a huge untidy spinnaker using the jib of an old yacht, patched like a longshoreman's breeches. At 10 a.m. we sighted Arensgund lightship on the bows. The wind going westerly again we had to take off the spinnaker, and hoisted our balloon instead of the staysail. At one o'clock we passed Arensgund lightship and met an American steamship, the St Anthony of

Tacona, with her flag at half-mast for President Harding's death.
We had a grand run into Helsingfors past Grohara under Sveaborg
and through the channel I had learnt last year, taking in our
balloon just before rounding into the Yacht Club harbour where
we anchored at 4.30.

We stayed two days in Helsingfors, and then, deciding to make
a short cruise among the islands, tried to wind up the motor,
which I had been told had been thoroughly overhauled in Reval.
It did not budge. I got a man to look at it and he found the pump
clogged with sand, and a spindle ruined. A new one had to be
made, and this took three days. In the meantime it blew so hard
that, remembering last year's difficulty, I funked having the yacht
swung, as I should have done, because owing to the fire we were
without the mattresses that alone had made it possible to save
her topsides during the operation last year. We decided to have
her swung in Reval, and made up our minds to cruise a little
way westwards among the islands, and then to go south.

Hexchen, from Reval came in the day after our arrival and we
were visited by a young lady of her crew, who, with the exception
of their professional sailor seemed to be the only person on board
with an understanding of ships. Two days before we left Hexchen
put to sea but woke us in the middle of the night by running us
down, her captain being very seasick. However, she did not do us
much damage.

Ransome was pleased to take Evgenia to Helsinki as she had missed
this part of the trip the previous year. They then cruised the Finnish
Archipelago to Rafsö, rode out the gale and, in a break in the weather,
returned to Estonia.

By the time they came to lay Racundra up for the winter Ransome's
account had returned once again to descriptive narrative:

Laying Up

The wind still continuing from the southwest, and the south cone
still swinging from the yard arm at the storm signal station, I
decided to lay up Racundra for the winter here, and, there being
no room on the Yacht Club mole, obtained permission from the
Estonian Government for Racundra to spend the winter in the
Government yard. I made my request in the morning and I had
scarcely returned on board when a diminutive tug arrived with an
enquiry as to our draught and the form of our keel, together with
an offer to tow us at once to the yard, which latter I refused as I
wished to get all things in order first and, besides was expecting
visitors on board. We made an appointment for the next day.

*Racundra was slowly lifted from the water,
and higher and higher into the air.*

We spent the afternoon removing all the running rigging that was
not needed for a last partial hoisting of the sails, and we loosened
the lacing except at the leech and luff. Next morning, for the first
time for many days we had sun and though the wind was rather
too strong for comfort we spread the sails enough to give them
a final drying. At three o'clock the little tug arrived, smaller even
than Racundra, and, casting loose from the mole, and getting our
anchor, we were presently through the harbour to the low swing
bridge, which separates the harbour proper from the Government
Dockyard. Here we waited an hour for the bridge to open, and
when it did, it did so rather grudgingly, so that, the tug starting
its engines in a hurry, we had a narrow escape from catching our
shrouds on the bridge end. This, however we avoided by an inch,
and were presently tied up to the quay between the lightship from
Nekmangrund which was noisily adjusting her fog siren, and two
old iron lighters. We then set to work to strip Racundra bare. We
took down the shrouds, and lay forlorn against the quay with
nothing but the masts standing. We slept there that night, and in
the morning a little crane came above us, and lifting the masts out
laid them on two trolley cars, together with the shrouds, dinghy,
oars, anchors and chains, and lifebelts. The crane then became
a locomotive, towed the trolleys to the shed where the stuff was
to be stowed, the Ancient and I following on foot, with bowed
heads, like principal mourners at a funeral procession.

That done, we were towed to a corner of the dock where we were
to be raised, and presently a gigantic crane pulled itself towards
us with wire ropes, till it hung, like a sort of angular octopus

Slowly it lowered Racunda onto an erection of timber balks.

above our heads. Two long strops were passed round Racundra, the crane began to work, and Racundra was slowly lifted from the water, and higher and higher into the air till she was swinging far higher than the roofs of the sheds about us. This as it was explained to me, was because the crane is charged for by time, and the higher the boat is lifted the longer it takes to lower it, so that money is made as it were at both ends. When the two blocks were almost touching, so that even if it had wished the crane could not possibly lift Racundra higher or extract more money from my pocket, it dragged itself against the bank and presently, ever so slowly, it lowered Racundra onto an erection of timber balks, where she lay steady on her flat keel. The strops still in place in case of accident, till props and wedges had been fixed about her, then the strops were removed, and the crane moved hungrily off to lift other boats and money. Tired out, partly perhaps with nervous strain of seeing our beloved one swing aloft among circling swallows instead of on the element to which she properly belongs, we climbed up a ladder into her and went to bed. The Cook went first, the Ancient muttering in his beard, "If it takes the Missus, there's nothing for us to fear."

Ransome recalled this period in his autobiography:

'There was no break and I was presently back in Riga, making Racundra ready for a cruise among the Finnish islands.

This was one of the pleasantest of our voyages. We made a slow passage to the Moon Sound, through the narrow gap in the Rohukulla Reef to the deserted harbour of Rohukulla. Then, after looking at some shallow-draught sailing boats (said to be copied from South American whalers that have for a hundred and fifty years been used at Hapsal), we went on to Reval and thence to Helsingfors, after which, happily cut off from letters, newspapers and all politics whatsoever, we took, now the inner, now the outer channels through the Finnish islands. We had a very fine grass-snake with us, and, though loath to part with him, we endowed him with an island very thickly populated by frogs. We ourselves lived for the most part on eggs that tasted of seaweed, milk that tasted of seaweed, and the fish that we caught while at anchor. The Gulf of Finland is fed by such large rivers that it is not very salty. The fish we caught were mostly perch and pike and very much better to eat than the same fish caught in ordinary fresh water. Here, in the Gulf, pike behave like salmon. In the winter when the streams are frozen, they go, like salmon, to the sea, and in the spring they come up the streams to spawn, such of them as evade the humans who are waiting for them with spears, traps and nets, to make 'golden caviare' of their roe and to dry good white fillets of pike-flesh in the sun. When the pike-run is on, you may see the pike alive in tubs in Reval market, and watch a housewife carrying one home still kicking in her shopping basket.

We brought Racundra back to Reval in September and, as I found urgent messages from the Manchester Guardian asking me to go into Russia, and a series of southerly gales set in, I arranged to lay her up there for the winter. We unrigged her, took everything out of her, and, with Eggers, her designer, watched her lifted from the water by a huge floating crane, watched her swinging high above our heads and set down on the quay as tenderly as if she were an eggshell. A wooden cradle was built for her. She was roofed in with planks to protect her from the snow. Evgenia and the Ancient went off by train for Riga and I left for Petrograd and Moscow to arrange with the Russians for the articles they were to write for an Economic Supplement to the Manchester Guardian that was being edited by J. M. Keynes.'

Appointed Honary Local Representative for Riga.

The Cruising Association

Arthur Ransome was a great friend of Herbert Hanson, one of the founders of the Cruising Association, the principle organisation for cruising yachtsmen. No doubt, because of their friendship, and the considerable interest in cruising that they both shared, Ransome joined the Association.

The Cruising Association Bulletin records that in early 1922, before Racundra was built, he joined the CA as a foreign resident, address c/o British Consulate, Riga, Latvia. He was appointed Honorary Local Representative for Riga in 1922 a position he retained until 1925 when he returned to England. His membership of the Association preceded that of his only other sailing organisation, the Royal Cruising Club, which he did not join until 1924.

Whilst Ransome was HLR for Riga he sent back reports for publication in the Bulletin.

In April 1922 he wrote reports on both Riga and Reval.

RIGA – There were a few days thaw some weeks ago and the ice below the Dvina bridges was broken up, so that it became possible to cross the river in a ferry steamer instead of sitting in a sledge propelled by an active fellow on skates. The steamers are still running just by the town, but there is a solid block of ice in the mouth of the river, and the ice has packed above it almost to the bridges. Navigation is not expected to open for another fortnight. Winter fishing, through holes in the ice, is still going on. On Sunday, though the snow was rather sticky, three ice-yachts were out on the Stint See where is the harbour and Club House of the Riga Y.C. Fitting out and painting have begun, however, and, though we only know of one new yacht being built, an epidemic of dinghies under construction is a healthy sign.

REVAL – Here too the winter has been a very hard one. Even the usually ice free Baltic Port (30 miles west of Reval) has been frozen for a short time this year. Navigation to Reval is proceeding with the help of ice-breakers, but at one time over a dozen ships were stuck in the ice between Cape Surop and Reval. The bay is still full of ice, and it is possible to walk out to the ships, although a year ago at this time, my own boat and several others were already afloat. The last few days of thaw have however brought owners and paint-pots to the mole in the harbour, where the boats of the two Clubs spend the winter. No building in Reval at present, but we hear of new boats in Parnau and Narva.

The new yacht he reported in Riga was his own Racundra completed in late August 1922.

In August 1922 he again reported on Riga and Reval.

RIGA – There are few cruisers here, probably because of the lack of harbours in the gulf, where a yacht leaving Riga has a hundred miles to go before reaching the narrow entrance to Moon Sund (extremely difficult, except under power, in some winds), scarcely less to Parnu or Arensburg, and no harbours on the way to any of these places, except Hainasch, on the Eastern coast, small and only partially protected. This year one yacht, Hansa, has gone to Finland, one, Ursula, to Reval, seven have made the trip to Runö Island and back (120 miles) and five made a four-day river cruise up the Aa to Mitau and back.

REVAL – The harbour for sailing ships is chock a block with schooners, and there is hardly a vacant berth along the moles. The Bollwerk, where are the two Yacht Clubs, is a fine sight with yachts moored all round it, like the petals of a daisy, including among several new boats a big cruising yawl from Germany, and an interesting Marconi rigged sloop from Finland, better fitted, however, for the sheltered waters of the Finnish skerries than for our open coast. Many boats have made the trip to Finland, Elisabet has gone to Stockholm, Gudrun to Kaspervik, and, while your correspondent was swabbing decks, he saw a little yawl (26 feet all over) come in with Swedish flag at the mizzen. The little ship was fifty years old, and her crew was older, two ancient school-masters from Wisby, in Gotland, who had made the passage direct, taking five days over it, adventurous Vikings, who looked warily round the harbour where they had never been before, and asked if it was safe to tie up, or whether they had better lie outside, as they had been told in Gotland that there were wild times in these parts.

February 1923 saw a brief note from Riga.

RIGA – There is skating on the yacht club harbour and ice-yachting on the lake. The winter has been mild. Though ice is floating down the river, the Gulf was still open in January and navigation for big ships was unimpeded.

In April 1923 Ransome sent an article to the Bulletin entitled 'Sailing in the Eastern Baltic'. In the article he refers several times to his voyage in Racundra the previous autumn.

SAILING IN THE EASTERN BALTIC.

The best time for small cruisers in the Eastern Baltic is from the last week in May to the end of July. As a general rule the few local yachtsmen who cruise, as apart from racing, bring their ships to their home ports by the beginning of August. Last year, sailing from Riga on August 20 (only because we could not get our boat into the water earlier) and returning on September 26, I did not meet a single yacht outside the sheltered waters of the various harbours. This is comprehensible, because the nights lengthen very rapidly and after the middle of August are extremely cold. Ice makes sailing impossible during a large part of the year. I broke my sailing dinghy out of the ice on Nov 4 in 1921, and took her ashore after sailing the previous day, and launched her again on April 28, bumping into submerged ice on our first sail. That, however, was a bad winter. The year before I was sailing on April 14. In the spring and at the back end of the year there is a good deal of violent weather, which in these waters very soon raises an uncomfortable sea. The weather changes with great rapidity, and for the most part seems easily able to keep pace with the barometer, which seldom has time to give one much warning. On the other hand, Midsummer, in spite of occasional mist and calm, usually means a month or six weeks on end of perfectly delightful weather, when, sailing at midnight, there is no need to light the binnacle lamp. I have been able at midnight to read the small type Oxford Vergil, lying on the cabin roof. At sea, though the sun does go below the horizon, you never lose the light, the glow of morning and evening are one, and just shift a little way along the skyline before the sun comes up again. Peculiarities of these waters? No tides, but in certain places among the islands strongish currents, which vary with the winds.

Sailing Directions? The Baltic Pilot (Parts I and II) while pessimistic in the extreme is indispensable for information about the larger ports. It has, however, a horrid habit of remarking about all the more interesting channels and harbours for small draught vessels: 'As this should not be attempted without local knowledge, no directions are given.' Charts? English and German Admiralty charts are best in a general way, though neither have been able to keep pace with the changes made by the war. These waters used to be Russian, and none of the small countries, Finland, Esthonia or Latvia, can afford the cost of a hydrographic department on the old scale. The Finns, however, have issued a number of delightfully printed and coloured charts of their coast, and the Esthonians have produced charts of the islands which should certainly be obtained by anyone cruising in this direction as they mark harbours and many land and sea marks which have not yet been recorded elsewhere. These can be obtained from the Harbourmaster, Sadama Kontor, Tallinn (Reval), Esthonia. Language? To be at home everywhere, one would need Finnish, Lettish, Esthonian and Swedish. One can get on quite well with Russian or German, and in the larger ports there is usually someone about with a good lot of English words acquired on British ships. In the larger ports, Riga, Reval, Helsingfors, one can buy all necessary food supplies but not always such things as blocks, shackles, etc. Of the three Helsingfors is best but not perfect. At Abö, further west along the Finnish coast, almost everything can be obtained. Away from the larger ports, milk, eggs, butter and potatoes can usually be bought though here the language difficulty becomes real. At a number of places on my Autumn cruise last year I found islanders who, for patriotic reasons, or else from necessity, refused absolutely to talk any language but their own Esthonian. Tobacco is the very devil to get. English tobacco is almost unobtainable, and, when you do find a stray tin of it, it is priced as if it were the Elixir of Life. Local tobacco, except in Helsingfors, is horrid except for the actual smoker, and only just tolerable by him for want of something else. Even local tobacco is sometimes not to be had. For some time I had to do with raw leaves given me by one of the lighthouse keepers and dried over the cabin lamp. Fishing? On some of the banks a stout fish like a cod is to be caught on a weighted spinner jerked up and down in four to six fathoms of water. Among the islands and off most of the harbours you can catch small fish called killos, like sprats. I caught a lot on fly, but when hungry went after them with a worm on a very small hook, one minute shot and a very light quill float thrown out to lie flat along the water. You give it a pull now and again to prevent it from hanging straight down, and strike at the first stab of the float. These little fish swim in shoals and take the bait in a petulant manner, ejecting it immediately, so that there is some sport in catching them, they make good soup and a really admirable fry. The water is not very salt and in many inlets perch and pike are to be caught in the usual ways. There are also small flat fish. There are any quantity of revoltingly oily sea duck.

The Gulf of Riga was swept for mines by a German flotilla last summer. A friend met one floating south of Runö Island in June, and in August I passed one at the entrance to the Worms Sound. Only a small area round Hainasch harbour, the northern coast of Esthonia, from Dagorot to Baltic Port, and the approaches to Petrograd are still coloured red in the Admiralty Mine charts. The year before last, five mines were washed into Sandy bay between Baltic Port and Reval, where I lay at anchor in the summer, my mainsail having been stolen by local pirates.

Further east much remains to be done in clearing mines, and ships going to Petrograd take a mine-pilot not far from Narva. Nowadays, however, there is very little risk in sailing between Riga, Reval and Helsingfors. To visit Russian ports, a special endorsement on ships' papers must be obtained from a Russian Consulate, and I am not at all sure that it would be given to a private yacht, sailing merely for pleasure. Esthonian, Latvian and Finnish Yacht Clubs are extremely hospitable to all members of recognised clubs. In Helsingfors the best moorings are those of the Nylands Club in the southern corner of the Southern Harbour. In Reval, the two clubs, the Estland and the Reval, have their buildings on an island mole in the harbour. There are mooring buoys for visiting yachts, and immediately after their arrival they are warped into places by the mole by the Yacht Club boatmen. In Riga, the visiting yacht must stop in the mouth of the river for examination. This, for a small boat, is often almost impossible, and it is best to anchor in the Winter harbour for clearance, thereafter proceeding up the river, either to the Livland Club, which is immediately opposite the town, or through the Mühlgraben, to the Stint Lake, where the Riga Club has an excellent private harbour. On leaving, yachts can clear either in the Mühlgraben, or in the town, but must hand over their tickets of leave to the officials at the mouth of the river. It is well to be very careful in declaration here. An unlucky yacht with a crew of German students was held up for some days owing to the accident of an unopened parcel handed on board just as they were leaving Germany and not entered in the stores list, turning out to contain a few bottles of schnapps. A. R.

His final report as Cruising Association Honorary Local Representative for Riga appeared In the December 1923 issue of the Bulletin.

RIGA – There have been only two weeks of spinnaker weather this season; the wind has gone widdershins round the compass. The signal station has worn out all its halyards hoisting one storm cone after another. Some say the Japanese earthquake had something to do with it. Others say that the weather is taking to politics and has been affected by the general unrest in Europe. Whatever the cause may be we are all agreed that with the exception of those two weeks at the end of June and the beginning of July there has been no summer sailing this year. Cruising, however, is undoubtedly looking up. Ursula came down from Reval for a regatta. Albatross came from Stettin. A big German yawl called here on her way to Petrograd, where her crew got into trouble. Ran and La Lune made good passages to Hangö, visited Abö and returned. Racundra went north again by Rohukulla, Reval, Helsingfors and Porrkala. All yachts are now laid up, but whereas last year the ice came before we were

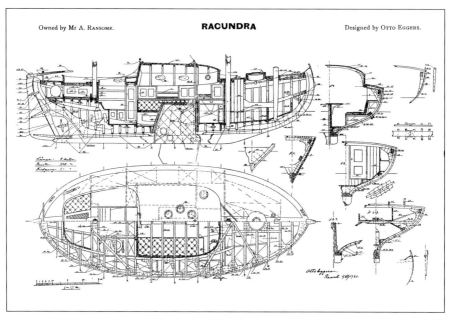

Owned by Mr A. Ransome.   **RACUNDRA**   Designed by Otto Eggers.

In February 1924 the plans appeared...

ready to use it, this year half a dozen ice-yachts are fitted out, and so far there has been no sign of ice. Sailing men who read in Blackwood's Magazine the account of the voyage of the Maid of Erin to Petrograd, will be sorry to hear that she was lost this year on the Finnish coast.

Also in this issue of the Bulletin was a review of Racundra's First Cruise. In it the reviewer suggested.

"Perhaps the Editor may wish to print her lines in a future issue".

Hanson obviously took notice and in February 1924 the plans appeared followed in April 1924 by the sail plans and lines.

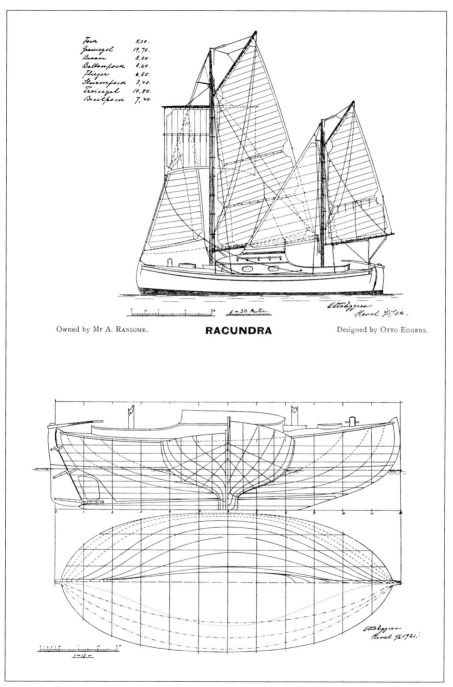

Owned by Mr A. Ransome.   **RACUNDRA**   Designed by Otto Eggers.

…followed in April 1924 by the sail plans and lines.

Getting Married

Early in 1924 Ransome's first wife Ivy (nee Walker) finally agreed to a divorce and, early in March, he came to London in order to finalise the arrangements. In a letter to Evgenia on the March 6th 1924 Ransome said:

'I have been to the Cruising Association's rooms, where there is a really fine collection of books on sailing, including RACUNDRA!!!!! I learnt there that several people are intending to sail to Riga and Reval this year because of the good time had in these

The love of his life, Evgenia.

ports by the cook and me!!! I only wish I had a photograph
of the cook's feet on the way back from Helsingfors'. (Evgenia
had a way of sticking her feet out in anger, when boats were becalmed
and engines wouldn't start and husbands were unsatisfactory.) 'However
I haven't and as everybody seems to think that we were all in
a permanent state of joy, unperturbed by weather or motor
and full of mutual admiration and affection, I don't undeceive
them and everyone who has a boat is dreaming of landing on
Runö and visiting the harbour of Heltermaa'.

Ransome was now, at last, free to marry the love of his life, Evgenia, and
preparations were made for the event to take place in Reval. On March
22nd he wrote to his bride to be:

The time of red floats is coming, and we will go after trout to
the Brasle, and take Racundra up to Mitau all by ourselves
and anyhow be together again and quite happy.

Has Juchter ordered my trysail?

I do so awfully wish I were back and that we were putting in the
three weeks residence in Reval that will be necessary before the
ceremony. During those three weeks we will be getting Racundra
into the water and rigged, and we will finally have a party on
board, consisting of Leslie and myself... oh yes, and you too.
We shall have to have you if only to make the tea. Of course
what will really happen is that you and Leslie will play cards,
and I shall sit on the deck in oilskins reflecting on life, and be
allowed in for tea when you have cleared the cards away.

Leslie was a former British Consul at Reval and a good friend of Ransome
and Evgenia.

On April 9th Ransome wrote to Evgenia with details of arrangements for
their marriage and finished with the words:

Tell Sehmel to varnish the fishing boat and put it in the water!
Make him get it ready at once so that it has time to dry.

They were married on May 8th by the British Consul at the Consulate
in Reval. His diary records the week of his marriage:

Consular fee stamps to the value of the fees charged must be

District of the British *Consul for Est*

1924. **Marriage** solemnized at *the British Consulate, Rev*

No.	When Married.	Name and Surname.	Age.	Condition.	Rank or Profession.	Re
	1	2	3	4	5	
7.	*Eighth May 1924.*	*Arthur Ransome,*	*40*	*Formerly the husband of Ivy C.G. Walker. spinster who obtained a divorce. Ransome J.E.G. against Ransome A.M. of 14/4/24.*	*Author*	*A*
		Evgenia Shelepin	*30*	*Spinster*	—	

Married in the *British Consulate, Reval,* _____ according to the

This Marriage was solemnized between us, { *Signed: Arthur Ransome,* }   in the Presence of us, { *Signed: Art* }

{ " *E. Shelepin* }   { " *Alm* }

I,   *H. Montgomery Grove*   , British *Consul-Gene*

That this is a true Copy of the Entry of the Marriage of   *Arthur Ransome*

in the Register Book of Marriages kept at this ——— *Consulate*

Witness my Hand and Seal this   *tenth*   *day of*   *M*

1924

Sunday 4th May
Heard cuckoo in the snow.

Monday 5th May
Typed Spring in the Eastern Baltic. 20 pp.
Rain.

Tuesday 6th May
Ledger 2 pp.

Saw Cross Bill 2 of them together with female of
dim dun colour.

Evgenia very angry because I locked the door and
forgot to shut it.
She was not well and I was an idiot.

to this form and cancelled.

Insert in this margin any Notes which appear in the original entry.

a   at   Reval

6	7	8
the time of Marriage.	Father's Name and Surname.	Rank or Profession of Father.
av, 17, eval	Cyril Ransome,	Professor at Victoria University
oga	Peter Shelepin.	Russian civil servant.

on Marriage Act of the year 1892 _____ by me,

lsey,   Signed: H. Montgomery Grove,

ttel,   HBM. Consul-General.

            at   Reval   , do hereby certify

Evgenia Shelepin,   Number   seven

        1924   H. Montgomery Grove

            H. B. M. Consul-General.

At the British Consulate Reval, the Master & Owner was married to the Cook.

Wednesday 7th May
Reval. Snow gone
Sails disappeared.
Wrote Robertson of ......

Long talk with Holst, who says Germans made
the Finnish civil war.

Thursday 8th May
At Brit. Consulate Reval the Master & Owner was married
to the Cook, who wore the flag of the Cruising Association.
Sails found.

Friday 9th May
Bonfire in forest. Put it out with snow.

Saturday 10th May
Paid £14 7s 0d for Racundra's wintering.
Racundra in water.

On May 10th Ransome wrote to his mother:

c/o The British Consulate,
Reval,
Esthonia.

May 10 1924

My dearest Mother

It is done. As a matter of fact it was done on May 8 at the
British Consulate, by His Britannic Majesty's Consul Grove, who
was extremely nice and welcomed Evgenia into the community
of British subjects with a really sweet little speech. After the
ceremony we went upstairs to Leslie's room, where Leslie had
left a bottle of champagne for this special purpose. Evgenia
recoiled from it in terror after half a small glass, but Grove
enjoyed it very much and would, I think, have felt that there
was something definitely missing if it had not been there.
So we have something to thank Leslie for even in absence, for
we should neither of us have ever thought of it for ourselves.

From the Consulate we rushed off to the shipyard carrying an
enormous tin barrel of paint, and found things going on very
well, from there we rushed to the train and just caught it, back
into the country. I came up this morning alone, getting up at
four to walk through the forest to the station, because today
Racundra goes into the water. E. follows on Monday to help in
putting her to rights inside, hanging up clock, barometer, etc.
Then provisioning, and then as hard as we can go for Riga,
where I want to leave her (the boat) while we go into Russia
for the Manchester Guardian. I shall collect all the material
for articles I can, and then if the weather is suitable we may
start for England, shedding articles into the post-boxes at all
the harbours on the way.

Racundra Returns to Riga

They left Reval for their homeport of Riga on the May 15th, taking with them Lt. Commander Gordon Steele V.C., an old friend of theirs, as crew. This passage was not a cruise in it's own right; it was delivering Racundra from her winter quarters to her home port on the Stint Sea.

Ransome recalls this passage in his handwritten deck log and also in a collection of typed up notes in a small loose-leaf notebook. He adopts the same style of narrative that was used when he recorded Racundra's third cruise.

May 15.
Left Reval 8.10 SW
Cleared Karlo 9.15. Wind WSW.
9.52 Wienes Lt in line.
11 turned round.
12.16 Wienes Lt in line ahead ENE. E $^1/_2$ N
by our compass.
2.30 Tied up YC buoy Reval.
Bar. fell to 28.8.

May 16.
Bar. 28.95 8.30 am. Wind westerly - calm.
S.E. storm signal hoisted but westerly wind prophesied
for tomorrow.
Hard red & gold sunset under cloud.
Bar. fell 28.85 12 pm.

Midnight. Barometer fallen one tenth to 28.85. S.E. storm signals over the harbour Captain's office, but local worthies prophesy a westerly wind for tomorrow. A hard red and gold sunset under cloud. We have however decided to start in the morning unless things are obviously against us, as I have to get the yacht to Riga where I must leave her while I go off to do some work.

> *May 17.*
> *Bar 28.65. Left Reval 4.10.*
> *Wind NE which held until Surop bore ESE three miles,*
> *time being 8.15.*
> *Sailed with wind aft. Calm & with change of wind*
> *SE & then to SW, fog. Land invisible.*
> *Bar. fell to 28.4 9 am.*
> *South wind from 5 in morning to 7.*
> *Sky cleared. Beat to windward. Entered Lahepe Bay.*
> *Wind dropped when we were near Pakerort.*
> *Motor started & stopped.*
> *My fault – lack of kerosene.*
> *Then wind increased steadily. We cleared Pakerort.*
> *Roogö. Snow on shore.*
> *Made Baltic Port 5.30.*
> *Tied up to schooner. Wind & rain.*
> *Bar. 11 pm 28.6 rising.*

Barometer fallen two more tenths to 28.65. But a N.E. wind. We weighed at 4.10 tacked out of the harbour, then with a beam wind sailed N.W. to clear Karlo point, which was invisible in mist. The wind held till 8.15. After rounding the point we had it almost dead aft, and as we cannot let out our boom as far as we should like, the after shrouds of the mainmast being set well back so that in all but hard gusty winds we can sail without bothering about the backstays, often a convenience when the helmsman is alone, we brought the wind first on one side and then on the other.

At 8.15 the mist thickened to fog. We got a glimpse of Surop light-house bearing E.S.E. and then the land became invisible, the wind fell away to nothing, wakened with a gentle puff from the S.E. and then freshened from the S.W. veering sixteen points in under three minutes. At 9 a.m. the barometer had fallen another two and a half points to 28.4. The force of the wind increased swiftly until it was lifting off the tops of the seas. Steele estimated it as force 5 for considerable periods to force 7. The sky cleared and we settled down to a long day on Racundra's worst point of sailing. The sea as usual here got up very quickly and battered at her head, flung lumps of itself on board, shifted the dinghy which was lashed down on the foredeck and made progress rather slow. We decided not to pinch her but to let her have as much as she wanted if only she would keep going, and, if towards evening we should find we were not going to get into Baltic Port by dark, to anchor in the bay on the eastern side of Surop.

The little harbour was full of schooners.

Racundra, thus put on her mettle, did her best. We took off the mizzen and left her full mainsail and staysail (our usual method of reducing sail) and she wallowed along very cheerfully. We tacked into Lahepe Bay and got the benefit of the smoother water bringing her out again close by Pakerort when for a moment the wind fell away. I tried to start the motor and it ran a few revolutions and stopped because I had omitted to open the main cock of the paraffin supply (I make this confession now because at the time I most unfairly said very hard things about the poor little donkey) but the mere suggestion of the motor seemed to have been enough for the wind, and it came at us again angrily enough to our great delight and we weathered Pakerort without difficulty, standing pretty far out (the buoys on the outlying shoals had not been replaced after the winter). There were great masses of snow on the northeast side of the cape, and the shores of the Roogö islands on the other side were white with big drifts. On the starboard tack we made the harbour mouth. We could see the little harbour was full of schooners and as we should be entering it with the wind abaft the beam I took in the staysail just before we went in, leaving us with the mainsail only under which Racundra is always ready to do anything we need in the way of manoeuvring. I was very glad we had no more sail for the little matchbox of a harbour was crammed with shipping, schooners lying two abreast on either side, and all other available berths being occupied with small cutters and skiffs and a fine wooden double ended motor ketch. Racundra waltzed demurely in the narrow lane between them until we had obtained permission to tie up alongside one of the schooners, when we dropped our anchor, for convenience in making sail again, and put her alongside, the schooner captain who greeted us with a broad smile an ingratiating manner and a flow of English swear words

(he having sailed on English ships and being fully persuaded
that he was in this manner doing the best that could be done to
make us welcome) giving us a hand with our warps. We had
entered the harbour at five thirty. At eleven p.m. the barometer
had taken a turn for the better and stood at 28.6 with
a tendency to rise.

> *May 18.*
> *Barometer 28.7. 9 am. Strong NW wind.*
> *28.9. 8 p m. SW cone signals.*
> *Harbour master produced telegram from Dorpat announcing*
> *the NW wind & saying that it would go to SW gale.*
> *We feeling lucky but still wet.*
> *Trees all bare & snow on Roogö.*
> *Bar. 29. 12 midnight.*

9 am. Bar. 28.7. Strong N.W. wind. S.W. storm signals up. The
harbourmaster, an old friend, showed us a telegram from the
meteorological observatory at Dorpat announcing this wind and
stating that it would turn to a S.W. gale. We decided to sit tight
and get dry. Steele and I explored the old fort of Peter the Great.
It was extremely cold, the trees all bare and the Roogö shore white
with snow. We gave the Cook a holiday and lunched on shore.

> *May 19.*
>
> *9 am. Bar. 28.85.*
> *Fishing at Tocusund. 4 pike between us.*
> *12 pm. Bar. 28.8*

Bar. 28.85. Wind S.W. We decided to visit my old fishing haunts
along the little river at the head of the bay. I hired a carriage,
a funny little rusty ancient thing with the stuffing of the cushions
coming through the leather, the wheels inclined to be either
bowlegged or knock kneed or to amputate themselves altogether,
and a driver who knew two or three words of Russian. We packed
this equipage with bait can, fishing tackle, knapsacks, fishing rods,
Steele and myself. It was one of those characteristic Russian
carriages built for one man or an affectionate couple, and each of
us had to keep in position by putting a foot on the step. The Cook
elected to make up lost time in sleep, and lent Steele her rod. We
had a jolly drive and saw a number of peewits, oxen ploughing,
yellowhammers, larks, and generally enjoyed ourselves. My old
wooden bridge under which there used to be big perch had gone

and a new stone bridge was being built. We crossed by a temporary bridge and a causeway of big stone, which nearly gave the coup de grace to our carriage.

We came back at twilight with four pike, two of which we gave to the schooner alongside. The other two we took with us, and that genius of a Cook made the most delicious pike cutlets and pike soup.

> *May 20.*
> *8 am 28.7 SE Cones*
> *Left Baltic Port 1.05. Wind NE 6. Sea 4. Swell 2.*
> *Blue cirrus cloud.*
> *1.48 C Westernas SE 3 cables.*
> *2.20 Arabusch S by E.*
> *5.5 Passed Sand Grund, no spar buoy, with breaking water.*
> *6 Spithamn 1 m. Course SSW.*
> *Wind changed to N 2-4. Worms beacons in line. S 27 W (SW by S $^1/_2$ S) S our compass. Steered for them. Course SSW.*
> *7.42 Telness beacon in line. S 20 E.*
> *8.36 Ramsholm beacon in line. Beacon on the Hestholm v. hard to see. Steele found them. Then spitways without brooms. Got the big beacon SSW of Hapsal light but could not in the dark get the Hapsal beacon.*
> *12.40 Anchored in 2 fathoms astern of schooner which came in before us, just off E of line of leading lights Pullapas. Very good pike supper.*
> *Bar. 28.96. 40 miles in $9^1/_2$ hours, average over 4 knots.*
> *Part of the time light air & being directly astern a much reduced area of canvas.*

Bar. 28.7. S.E. cone up. We were undecided as to whether or no to get on, but when the day cleared with a good wind from N.E., a blue sky with cirrus, we decided to get round to Hapsal if we could, where, even if the S.E. did prevent us from getting through the Sound we could get good shelter at Rohukulla and amuse ourselves by investigating beacons. Shopping delayed us a little and it was one o'clock before we left Baltic Port. Wind N.E. force 6 (Steele's estimate). Sea 4. Swell 2. We made good headway passing Cape Westernas at 1.48. Cape Arabusch with its lonely little tree at 2.20. None of the sparbouys were yet in position, but we could see a solitary rock on Gras Grund to the north of us, and at 5.05 passed Sand Grund on which every now and then we saw the white fountain of breaking water. At 6 we rounded Spithamn, one mile distant, with its row of windmills. Two schooners were anchored on its western side and a third was being built in a gap among the great pines.

As we rounded the point the wind backed to the North. We sailed
S.S.W. and presently got Worms beacons in line, and kept them
so till 7.42 when we got the Telness Beacons in line bearing S.20.E.
giving us a good fix of our position. None of the buoys marking the
shoals being in position. At 8.36 we got the beacons and Ramsholm
in line and altered course to keep them so. We found it very hard to
get the beacons on the little island of Hestholm on the other side of
the Worms Nukke Channel, but spotted them luckily just in time as
it was getting too dark to see the few temporary spars without tops
to them which were all that were marking the narrowest part of
the channel. We followed their leading line until we got the lights on
the southern side of Hapsal bight in line when we knew we were
through the worst of it. I know no more puzzling channel than this,
which in places is so narrow that you can throw a stone across it
without an effort and runs close by visible rocks with a tempting
stretch of apparently open water on the other side where the
shoals are a few feet under water. It was now so dark that strain
our eyes as we might we could not see the beacons by Hapsal town
that mark the other narrow channel between the sands leading up
to the pierhead. The dim ghost of a schooner crossed our bows far
ahead and we decided to follow her, but it was clear that she too
could not see the beacons for she presently came up into wind and
anchored. We sailed close under her stern and then held on,
sounding with the lead till we found two fathoms, when we
anchored a little to east of the line of the big leading lights on the
south shore and out of the channel. 10.40 p.m. 40 miles in $9^{1}/_{2}$
hours. The Cook had made a magnificent pike supper for us, and
we had a hot rum and turned in to wait for dawn, keeping the
halyards on the sails. Bar. 28.96. We should have made better
speed if we had had our square sail as with the wind directly aft
the position of our boom means that the effective area of canvas
is greatly reduced.

May 21.
4 Bar. 28.95.
As soon as beacons visible, made sail.
We had anchored S of channel.
4.30 Weighed. Wind NNW.
6.10 Through Rukeraga.
7 Bar. rising.
8 am 29.1.
8.15 Worms beacons in line.
9.25 Slava wreck ESE. Moon High Beacon S by E. $^{1}/_{2}$ E.
9.42 Moon Channel bearing SSE.
11.55 Paternoster bearing W by N. Streamed log 1.3.

Sailed S 30 W. 7.1.
1.25 Booms over. Course S 40 E. Log 8.4.
5 Booms over. Course S 20 W. Log 20.8.
6.35 Wind backed to W
7.40 Sighted Runö bearing SW.
9.20 Started engine. Log 28.

4 am. Bar. 28.95. Beacons visible. Made sail and had breakfast, porridge and coffee. Wind N.N.W. 4.30 weighed. We had a little difficulty in following the channel owing to the absence of the usual buoys, but sailed up to the entrance of Rohukulla harbour where I wanted to have another good look at the leading marks, and made for the Rukeraga passage, where at the narrowest part, only a few yards in width, where nothing but a centreboard dinghy could tack, we were glad to find three pairs of sparbouys, though we did not need them, steering by keeping the Rohukulla beacons in line over the stern. At 6.10 we were through the Rukeraga. Sailed S.S.W. to pick up the beacons on Worms, which are like huge corkscrews and quite unmistakeable.

Got them in line at 8.15. At 9.25 the wreck of the old battleship Slava bore E.S.E. Soon after we got the beacons on Shildau island in line, rounded the corner of Moon Island and steered for Werder lighthouse between Werder lighthouse and Paternoster on its little island. At 11.55 we were through the Moon Sound. Paternoster bore W. by N. Streamed the log reading 1.3. Course S. 30 W. 1.25 brought the booms over. Log 8.4. Course S. 40. E. At 5 brought the booms over log 20.8. Course S. 20 W. The wind backed to the W. At 7.40 sighted Runö island in the middle of the gulf bearing S.W. The high land with tall trees and the lighthouse make it visible a long way and we estimated the distance at 12 to 15 miles, but distances had been hard to judge all day owing to persistent mirage. The wind fell away to nothing and remembering the harbourmaster's warnings that a southerly wind would certainly follow, we decided to call upon the little donkey. It started at the first touch, as if it had been waiting to show that it felt no ill will for the insults that I had unjustly heaped upon it when I had asked it to work without paraffin and we steamed the whole of the rest of the way. Racundra is a heavy ship and the little donkey only pretends to four horse power so that our speed was not great. However we kept moving steadily. I got an hour's sleep, and then took over, for the night. There was a fine explosive sunset, throwing up spurts of red flame-like clouds, and just at sunset a schooner, with a square topsail set, passed silhouetted against the glow. There was a grand moon.

May 22
Turned out Steele at 3 am. Slept till 5.30.
At night schooner with square topsail. Steamer going N.
Moonlight. Sunset like an explosion, red spits of cloud.
Little engine going v. well.
Bar. 7 am 29.25.
9.23 Riga High Lt. S by W Log 50 + 17.2.
10.15 R.H. Lt. became church. Altered course SSE until:
Sighted Riga 2.30. v. slight NW wind & calms all day.
6.35 Between piers. The bridge and the shallows dredging.
10.45 Anchored in Sport Verein. Bar. falling.

Steele took over at 3 a.m. and I went below to thaw, and slept
till 5.30. 7 a.m. Bar. 29.25 very slight N.W. breaths but for the
most part calm. The little donkey going beautifully.

9.23 sighted land, a thin spire which we took for Riga high
light though it bore S. by W. and sorely upset my calculations.
We steered for it until 10.15 when it became an unmistakeable
church and we did our best to get back on our old course.
At 2.30 we sighted the thin white pillar of Riga lighthouse,
and a group of chimneys.

Presently we got the red lighthouse on the eastern mole and
then the howling buoy, two miles out, glittering in its new spring
paint. Dredgers were busy in the channel over the bar, and the
drawbridge of the great section of the bridge over the Dvina that
had been carried away by the ice was aground on the shallows.
At 6.35 we passed between the moles and were in the river. We
steered close by the Customhouse pier and our guard jumped on
board as we sailed past. We were given orders to proceed to the
Stint See harbour and there await clearance. In the Mühlgraben
however our guard thought better of it and asked us to put him
ashore when he would arrange that we should be cleared there.
We went alongside the stage and he disappeared. We waited an
hour and a half, and then, as it was getting dark and we had yet
to pick our way into the Stint See and find our little harbour, we
gave him up as a bad job and cast off. We could just see our way
into the lake but had a hard job of it trying to find our little bay,
where at 10.45 we anchored, in pitch dark and after supper
were lulled to sleep by the loud croaking of innumerable frogs.
Excluding the six hours anchorage at Hapsal we had made our
passage from Baltic Port to the mouth of the Dvina in 48 hours.
Distance about 160 sea miles. No great speed certainly but good
enough. None of the local boats had put to sea and we were in
time to witness their first regatta on the lake.

May 23.
Bar. 29.

The next day we went round to Riga town, coming up the river under sails and motor against a strong wind and current. In Riga town our Bosun (as Lieut. Commander Steele was described by the harbour police on the certificate they gave him) left us to return to Reval, and at dawn on the day after I sailed Racundra home again to the little harbour and the frogs, with whom alas she must keep company until I return from a journey into the interior.

It should be noted that the modern practice of using mb. for atmospheric pressure, 360 degrees compass rose for directions and the 24 hour clock were not then in use.

In his autobiography Ransome recalls this period and briefly mentions Racundra's Third Cruise:

'A few days later we went to Reval to get Racundra ready for sea after the winter ashore. It was cold and when we went to visit our friends in Lodenzee we found still a lot of snow in the forest round the house. On May 8, my divorce being completed, the Master of Racundra was married to the Cook at the British Consulate in Reval.

After a slow but pleasant cruise back to Riga, with Lieutenant-Commander Gordon Steele, V.C. as extra hand, we both went to Russia and spent a month in and around Moscow. Back in Riga I was busy writing articles for the Manchester Guardian, driving once a week up into the Lettish hill-country with my friend John Chapman of the American Consulate in Riga to fish two delightful little rivers, the Aniat and the Brasle, which were packed with trout and grayling. We used to spend the night in a peasant's hut, where the fleas were so hungry that we had no difficulty in getting up early and used to be fishing by 4.30 in the morning.

On August 1 we took Racundra for a leisurely cruise in the lower reaches of the Dvina, up and down Aa and up Bolderaa to that fascinating, mysterious, romantic and claustrophobic maze of shallow narrow channels winding between enormously tall and strong reeds for what feels like thousands of square miles. We lived mostly on eggs and the fish we caught. We sailed only for an hour or two at a time, as I had a lot of writing to do. By September 10 we were back in Stint See preparing to lay Racundra up for the last time, and on November 14 we said a sad farewell to her and to Riga, and sailed for England.'

This is the only published reference to Racundra's Third Cruise.

Postscript

Following the completion of the cruise the Ransomes decided to leave Latvia and return to England. They laid up Racundra for the last time and on the November 14th said a sad farewell to her and to Riga, and sailed for home. The purchase of a cottage at Low Ludderburn in the Lake District meant that Racundra had to be sold. The cost of the property and alterations had made a large hole in Ransome's savings, nothing else would have made him give up his idea of sailing Racundra to England or parting with his dream ship.

She was advertised in Yachting Monthly magazine for sale at £300. A young Adlard Coles, at that time a young and successful yachting author, expressed interest and offered £150 cash plus £100 guaranteed. After much exchange of letters and telegrams Coles offered £220 cash. The purchase was agreed on the July 4th. Ransome had assumed that Coles meant £220 cash and £30 guaranteed. A condition of the purchase was that Coles could not use the name Racundra (Adlard was planning to write a book on the voyage from Riga to England). The boat was renamed Annette II and the published book was Close Hauled. In consideration of this and to avoid a bitter row Ransome waived the additional £30.

Ransome provided Coles with information and assistance:

The Ancient will rig and get Racundra ready for sea in a very few days AFTER your arrival. It is quite useless to tell him to do anything before you arrive, as he simply won't do it. He will ship with you for the passage to England if he likes you, not otherwise. He is called Captain Sehmel by me. Other people address him less respectfully and get less out of him. He is an extremely charming old man, and makes himself very useful. You would have to come to some agreement with him about payment, privately, so as to avoid having articles made etc. Of course, you would have to send him home at the end of the trip. . . You will get no navigational assistance from him. He is incapable of reading a chart and though a first-rate rigger and admirable seaman, is a very old man. I never let him stand a night watch alone. You would have to pay him a pound or two a week, and naturally (you) would not discharge an old man in a foreign port without sending him home to the dinghies and little boats by looking after which he keeps alive.

In the event Sehmel did not sail to England with Coles.

Ransome also gave some advice about dealing with Customs:

You anchor, ready for sea, in the Club harbour and the Customs Officials will come from the Customs House at your request and make a pretence of looking over the ship. You give them a drink of the local spirit (vodka) in the cabin and a ham sandwich (this is important) whereupon they stamp your passports and give you a paper ticket which you have to give up at the mouth of the river to a ruffian who will wave at you from a small pier close by the big lighthouse on the port hand going down. Having handed over their ticket, you are free.

After returning to England Coles wrote to Ransome to thank him and enclosed a cheque for £10 towards the outstanding amount. It was never paid in. A short time after the boat was again up for sale and even offered to Ransome for £350! She remained in British waters under various owners until purchased by J.M. Baldock MP, who owned her for approximately 20 years. In 1976 ocean sailor Rod Pickering purchased her. He had discovered her in a bad state of repair in Tangier harbour. He carried out considerable renovation and sailed her across the Atlantic to the West Indies where she regrettably foundered on a reef north of Caracas.

No doubt she was 'unwilling yet to accept the idea of a final resting place'.

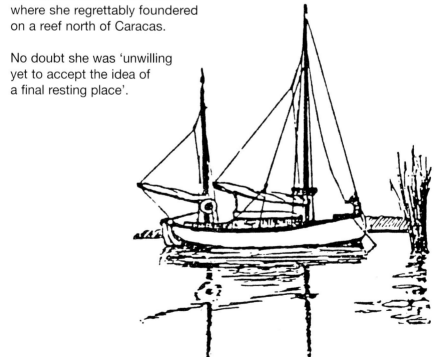

Acknowledgements

The research and publication of Racundra's Third Cruise would not have been possible without the help and assistance of a great many people. I particularly acknowledge the following:

My father, Ted, for giving me a copy of Swallows and Amazons for my 10th birthday, thereby introducing me to Ransome and sailing, both becoming a lifelong interest and passion. Alan Lawrence's article in the 1996 edition of Mixed Moss, the journal of the Arthur Ransome Society, made me aware of the cruise and inspired me to further research. Peter Cockayne of Chelmondiston, who, at an early stage, obtained copies of up to date maps of the area from his contacts in Riga.

Writers of books on Ransome: Peter Hunt, Jeremy Swift, Hugh Brogan, Ransome's biographer, and particularly Roger Wardale and Christina Hardyment for their help and encouragement. I have drawn heavily on the work of these writers during the preparation of the Prelude.

My friends at the Cruising Association for allowing me to use information from their archives. In particular my wife, the General Secretary, Ted Osborn, for proof reading and advice, Fay and Graham Cattell, for taking photographs of the area for me, finding detailed local maps, and assisting my research during my cruise of the Baltic in summer 2000, Arnis Berzins, the current HLR for Riga, for giving me a copy of the 1924 edition of the Latvian Yachtclub Yearbook, and Michael Howe, the CA's librarian, for allowing me access to items normally kept under lock and key.

I owe an incredible debt to the Special Collections Department of the Brotherton Library, University of Leeds, particularly Ann Farr and Suzanne Oakes, for permission to use Ransome material and photographs for which they hold the copyright.

Ransome's Literary Executors for permission to embark on the project and use his previously published and unpublished work. Various members of the Arthur Ransome Society, with special thanks to Ted Alexander and Dave Sewart for their enthusiastic encouragement.

Finally, Tim Davison of Fernhurst Books for suggesting publication and enabling me to complete the project.

Brian Hammett,
Blackmore, Essex.

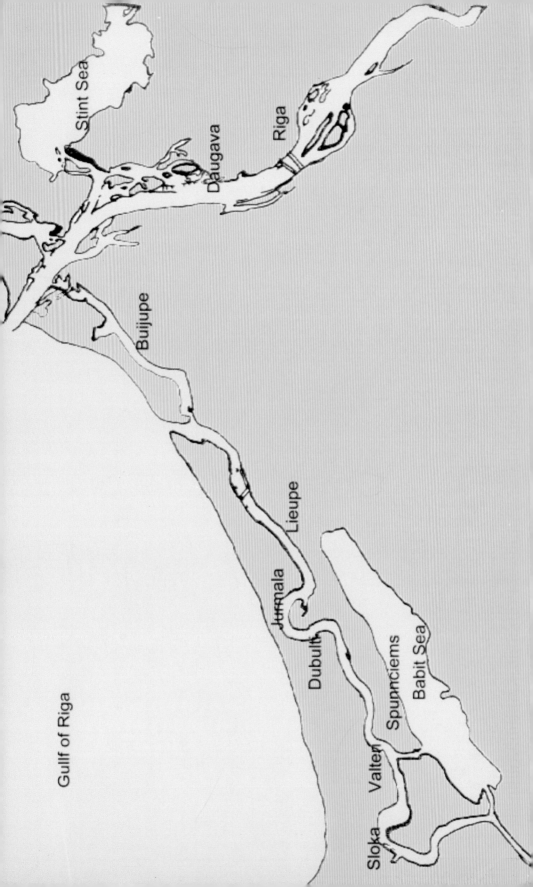